SCIENTIFIC MANAGEMENT IN RU~~SSIA~~

WORLD-CLASS SCHOOLS AND SCHOLARS

By

GRIGORIY Z. SHCHERBAKOVSKIY

Book 2.   N.A. Vitke and his Concepts

Science editor and author of preface: Prof. E.B. Koritskiy, Doctor of Economics

ISBN: 978-0-692-95192-7

NEW YORK, NEW YORK
2017

TABLE OF CONTENTS

Preface

The first book in Professor Scherbakovskiy's project, on A.K. Gastev and his school, is already in print. This second volume deals with N.A. Vitke, another outstanding Russian management scholar. In contrast to Gastev, he had no school of his own; nevertheless, his ideas attracted numerous gifted followers who deserve to be remembered.

As noted in the first book, the idea of social engineering was among the most substantial concepts proposed by Gastev. However, he never interpreted it with sufficient clarity. It was Vitke who picked up this concept and developed it in a scientific way. He was arguably the first in the world to treat management as social engineering in a way that is still relevant.

The book demonstrates how Kremlin economists and ideologists viciously attacked this view. Vitke's defeat, however, was a Pyrrhic victory for the Bolsheviks who consequently failed to offer any meaningful theoretical or applied achievement in management for decades.

In the meanwhile, these decades in the West saw robust progress in scientific management. Some revolutionary concepts developed over this period changed scientific management in a major way. Classical theories by Taylor, Ford, Fayol, Weber, and others were succeeded by behaviorist ones elaborated by Mayo and his followers such as Follett or Roethlisberger. They addressed the flaws in classical theories by taking full account of the "human factor", i.e., various aspects of social interactions, personal motivation and values, power and authority, leadership, communications and so on. Maslow came up with the famous "hierarchy of needs", Chester Barnard proposed an informal organizations theory, and F.

1

Herzberg developed his theory of motivation. In the following years the West laid the groundwork for the buoyant development of the qualitative approach and the systems approach, to name a few. Indeed, the greatest progress in scientific management was made precisely in the area banned by Bolsheviks. One only has to regret that Russian scientific management was separated from these new trends by the iron curtain and doomed to lag behind by more than half a century.

In accordance with the project concept, Vitke's main publication ("Organization of Management and Industrial Development", Moscow, 1925) is included in this book to give the reader a chance to appreciate Vitke's groundbreaking ideas first-hand. This paper, out of print since 1925, is published in a slightly abridged version. Professor Scherbakovskiy in his analysis and comments should be commended for putting Vitke's ideas in a modern context rather than merely retelling them.

I hope that everyone interested in scientific management and its history will benefit from this innovative and well-written treatise.

E. B. Koritzkiy

Introduction

On an August day in 1922, a steamer from Australia arrived at the port of San Francisco. A rather young gentleman came ashore with a university diploma in philosophy, ethics and psychology, a few published research papers and about 50 pounds sterling. He was George Elton Mayo, now regarded as the founder of "human management", a true revelation in the theory and practice of industrial organization.

A talented researcher, this native of South Australia became pretty famous in the USA after just a couple of years. In 1926 he became a professor and head of the industrial sociology department at Harvard School of Business where he worked until retirement in 1947. He owes his true world fame, however, to the legendary Hawthorn studies that helped him formulate a new approach to management in "The Human Problems of an Industrial Society" (New York, 1933) and "The Social Problems of an Industrial Society" (Boston, 1945).

What is the core of this new theory? The classical systems of scientific management by Taylor, Ford, Fayol and other pioneers that prevailed in the first quarter of the XX century, as is well-known, were dealing primarily with structural and economic factors of labor productivity. Mayo surely did not deny the importance of organizational structure or financial incentives in management. However, he saw a gaping hole in these classical systems, since they all but ignored the *social aspect* or *the human factor,* something at least as significant. If Taylor assumed that workers were concerned only with "making more money" and thought of them as robots (or even "buffaloes"), Mayo believed that every person was *unique.* His theory was based on the principle of individual differences. He claimed that workers were individuals and any management theory that calls for their uniform treatment would not be a true success.

The large-scale Hawthorne studies that covered 20 thousand workers made Mayo realize that work can hardly be reduced to "making a living". People need a more sophisticated motivation. They want to be treated as individuals, with attention to their personal or family problems that can impact their performance, they want to work in a good team. These experiments demonstrated that a good socio-psychological climate at workplace, as well as the team spirit do improve performance.

Mayo used this evidence for a far-reaching revision of the management function. At that time managers, in full accordance with Fordism and Taylorism, focused on organizational and economic problems. Mayo argued that their main objective was to deal with the *"diagnostics" of human relations in collectives and to strive for social harmony, foster a positive climate that would stimulate progress.*

Mayo's concept started a new era in scientific management and laid a foundation for a variety of behaviorist theories in this field. Dozens of books and hundreds of articles about his work, including those in dictionaries and encyclopedias, have been published.

We could certainly write more about Mayo and his ideas, but this book has a different subject. Mayo had a forerunner in Russia whose name was Nikolay Vitke. Several years before the Hawthorne studies he formulated a similar philosophy whose future, regrettably, turned out to be bleak. Indeed, his discoveries were made in a different system of geographical as well as political coordinates. The authoritarian Bolshevik regime was hostile to any "human management." The remarkable concept by a talented researcher was crushed by "Communist NOT experts" and consigned to oblivion. As opposed to Mayo, Vitke is hardly referred to in any encyclopedias and even the ubiquitous Internet seems to know little about this scholar. No books or papers by Vitke have been published since the second half of the 1920s. Most likely, the

4

founder of the "human management" theory fell victim to purges.

Since we hardly know anything about his biography, and speculations in this situation would be inappropriate, let us share a few guesses based on his publications.

Vitke obviously had a good education and a command of at least two foreign languages (English and French), as evidenced by the list of references in the original language cited in his principal book "Organization of Management and Industrial Development" (Moscow, 1925). Also, Vitke had a brilliant literary style that differed sharply from that of most Russian NOT scholars. Finally, many of his thoughts betray a background in philosophy, political economy and sociology.

At the same time, Vitke was anything but an armchair scientist. His theories and hypotheses were inspired by daily management practices. In fact, Vitke held a ranking position at the headquarters of the NOT movement in the USSR, the Central Control Commission and the Workers' and Peasants' Inspectorate (CCC-RKI), as the head of the Standardization Department. According to A.K. Gastev, serious application of scientific management in government agencies started only after this department had been established. Once converted by Vitke to the administrative technology division, it became "the most valuable, active and creative part of the governance reforms department at RKI."[1]

As for Vitke's political views, he certainly was a member of the Party, since otherwise it would be inconceivable to hold an executive position at the CCC-RKI, an agency once headed by Stalin, Kuybyshev, Ordzhonikidze and other ranking Communists. We doubt, however, that he was an orthodox Bolshevik. The spirit of his "human relations" concept was clearly too democratic to be compatible with Bolshevik ideas on management under the dictatorship of the proletariat. This is why we believe his affiliation with the Party was rather formal. Indeed, Vitke's numerous foes had every

---

[1] See Scherbakovskiy G.Z., Scientific Management in Russia: World-class Schools and Scholars. Book 1. "A.K.Gastev and TsIT". Frankfurt-am-Main, 2014, P. 129-130.

reason to accuse him of forsaking Marxist-Leninist ideals and "slipping" towards the views advocated by "bourgeois" scholars such as Fayol or Taylor. Rozmirovich, Vitke's most ruthless critic, snarled that while "methodologically wrong from the Marxist point of view, Vitke's philosophy was essentially void and useless if not outright harmful in practice." Nevertheless, she admits, it is presented in an apparently compelling format that employs Socialist rhetoric and quotes from Marx and Lenin; in particular, Vitke insists that the Soviet environment is much more favorable for its implementation than the bourgeois Europe. Ironically, Rozmirovich may indeed have a point about Vitke's presentation style.

This is essentially all we can say about the protagonist of this book. Let us now discuss the principal aspects of the theory developed by Vitke and his supporters.

Part I. The new scientific school and its destiny

Chapter 1. N.A. Vitke, Scientific Management as "Social Engineering"

As we have already mentioned, a new informal school led by N.A. Vitke took shape in Russia by mid-1920s. Its proponents such as Ya.S. Ulitskiy, S.D. Strelbitskiy, R.S. Mayzels and G.A. Nefedov supported Vitke's concept of management that he often referred to as "social engineering".

The term "social engineering", as we demonstrated in our first book, was first used by A.K. Gastev. However, Gastev's "social engineering" regarded a work organization as a *set of separate individuals* each of whom was subject to targeted managing influence. This interpretation focused on an individual worker, his work motions and time spent on them, his performance and output, the rate and pay system and so on.

In contrast to Gastev's concept that was largely based on ideas proposed by Taylor, the new theory relied on the *preeminence of collective rather than individual* nature of a work organization. Management was assumed to affect primarily the entire work collective, which was not interpreted as a simple group of individual workers but rather as a *social organism requiring cooperation among these workers.* A worker was thus compared to a biological cell that is certainly necessary, yet not self-sufficient.

The new concept instantly triggered vivid discussions that ended in a total defeat of its supporters. The insightful theory developed by Russian researchers was relegated to oblivion, and hardly any literature on this subject can be found.

We are most certain, however, that the verdict pronounced at that time on this school must be reversed.

Vitke and his like-minded colleagues, as opposed to mainstream management experts in Russia, identified three principal areas of NOT:

1. Problems of *the most efficient use of mechanical tools* belong to industry and need to be addressed by mechanical engineers.

2. The *improvement of the work process as an interaction between man and material production factors* may be called NOT as such. The issues it covers are the most efficient use of labor (selection methods, work motions and the like). These objectives, while not entirely alien to sociology, are reached primarily by means of psychology and physiology.

3. Since every worker maintains close ties with fellow men, human relations also may and should be subject to improvement. That is, the most efficient system of cooperation has to be developed. This third area represents *scientific organization of management* (SOM) or *social engineering* and employs methods of social psychology and other social sciences. Vitke and his supporters focused their research precisely in this field.

Before the war and the October revolution, Vitke wrote, NOT work was restricted to industry and the tasks formulated in pp. 1 and 2. Problems from the third area, even if raised, were handled by empirical means without any methodological or scientific analysis.

The military crisis in 1914 and subsequent years greatly exacerbated all problems of social organization and ultimately gave a strong impulse to the development of the third area of NOT, i.e., SOM or social engineering, whose principal subject is management as such and administration as its main function (Vitke called it "administrative engineering"). "Management studies left the confines of industry to spread to trade, banking and other institutions; administration and cooperation among workers were identified as a field of social relations. Much like physics and chemistry brought down the scientific thought from the heights of metaphysical speculations to make it work for agriculture and industry, much like biology now serving the needs of, say, animal husbandry, social sciences now cannot afford to be limited to broad deliberations on law and ethics, evolution of family or the theory of progress. They have been drawn into the midst of practical issues handled by the administrator and should help him properly organize correspondence, place desks in the office, write a business letter, set up a system of accounting and reporting, and (the most important help!) educate the administrator in the spirit of genuine cooperation with his social mechanism."[2]

Therefore, according to Vitke, social engineering is an area of NOT that focuses on human interactions in the overall work process and explores ways and means of affecting these interactions in order to achieve optimum performance.

Note that followers of the social organization school, being keenly aware of the ever-increasing role of administration in industrial progress, held that sound organization was even more critical to industry than any technological breakthroughs. For instance, Mayzels wrote: "It is safe to say that while the 19th century is reasonably called that of steam and electricity, the 20th century will be known as that of rational organization."[3] Time has proven this forecast to be accurate. Vitke shares some intriguing thoughts on this subject.

He argued that as manufacturing tools concentrate and become more efficient and sophisticated (with the development of "industrialism", to use his own term), labor becomes more and more collective, which means labor management plays a more prominent role. While management

---

[2] See: Vitke N.A., Scientific organization of management technology *(Nauchnaya organizatsiya administrativnoy tekhniki)* / The Beginning of NOT. Forgotten Discussions and Ideas that Never Came to Life. [*U istokov NOT: Zabytye diskussii i nerealizovannye idei*]. Leningrad, 1990, p. 164.
[3] Mayzels R.S., Management and Organization of Agencies. *(Upravlenie i organizatsiya uchrezhdeniy).* Moscow-Leningrad, 1926, p. 7.

was very primitive in the era of small business, he maintains, its impact becomes much stronger in the industrial era.

A modern factory manager can ill afford to act like a small business owner, i.e., pretend to be more experienced and knowledgeable than any of his subordinates with respect to any specific problem that comes by. Industrial management now calls for closer attention and thorough analysis. It can no longer rest on *personal discretion,* since modern manufacturing has become too broad and complex, and every partial worker is too specialized, each and every operation must be too meticulously calculated and planned.

Industrialism has led today's large-scale manufacturing to an **organizational crisis** caused by the struggle between the unfolding cooperative nature of labor and the restraints imposed on it by the traditional individualistic management (the isolated worker system), a legacy of small business. This crisis has shattered personal discretion as the basis of management.

Vitke suggests that this crisis can be resolved by *"an organizational revolution"* that "affects not only relations among things and those between things and humans, but also relations among people involved in the production process." [4] In other words, this revolution extends to *the social organization* as well as the organization of technology.

The cooperative nature of a large modern company, he maintains, calls for strict planning of all elements of the labor process by partial workers as well as for *sound organization of people as participants in integrated work cooperation.* While abolishing *personal discretion* as the principle of individualistic management, the organizational revolution also destroys *individualistic micro-management,* as well as the opposite pole of this system, i.e., *blind obedience by the worker.*

The simple old formula of *a specific order followed by specific execution* was *the true axis of management* at a small

---

[4] Vitke N.A., Organization of Management and Industrial Development. *(Organizatsiya upravleniya i industrialnoe razvitie.)* Moscow, 1925. p. 40.

factory from top to bottom. Industrialism offers a far more modern pattern of relations within the collective labor process. Industrialism flatly rejects all the attitudes and skills of an isolated worker. "A modern enterprise is organized by means of strict accounting and planning rather than personal discretion. It replaces direct orders and supervision by a corporate work system, rigorous collective labor routines, automatism of collective labor and fostering collective ownership with regard to the production process."

Therefore, as he emphasized on many occasions, the organizational revolution in industry has evoked the cooperative nature of large-scale production. While consistently applying the accounting and planning principle to the manufacturing process "as a whole", it *goes much further by commanding human relations in the manufacturing process and transforming the authoritarian individualistic management style into a fundamentally different system of collective labor cooperation.* This new system aims at nurturing *"the spirit of the hive", i.e., the interest in completing the task by every team and by the entire work collective.*

The cornerstone of Vitke's theory is **the sound organization of relations among workers as members of integrated work cooperation**, which means he clearly distinguished two kinds of management – that of people and that of things – and focused on the former.

"Management," he wrote, "is a skill of combining people's wills (as opposed to intellects) so that various tools are properly used to achieve the specific objectives of an organization."[5] Management is essentially the art of organizing and directing human wills.

This activity must evidently stem from scientific knowledge whose advantage over the empirical approach hardly needs to be proven. This reliance on science, Vitke believed, was especially critical for Russia who had to rebuild

---

[5] Vitke N.A., Scientific Organization of Management: Speaking Notes. (*Nauchnya organizatsiya upravleniya*). In "Scientific Management" (*Nauchnaya organizatsiya tekhniki upravleniya*). Moscow, 1924, p. 3.

11

its economy after the tumultuous revolution. The point is not only that the revolution shattered the government and the economic system to replace the destroyed edifices with haphazard and ill-conceived barracks of new administrative and economic agencies. The point is not only that the new "organic" stage of the revolution now calls for persistent and scrupulous efforts to develop the most sound and economical system of permanent government agencies and therefore needs scientific administration.

These are just technical problems. The main point is that the new government and the new economy have to be built using new people, in a new environment and for unprecedented new purposes. In this situation, reliance on pre-revolutionary experience only would be fundamentally wrong, though this experience should not be ignored completely. The only reliable policy here is to use scientific management and administrative engineering,

There is much more to building new organizations by new people in a new environment than simply making adjustments for the new social and political system. Following Gastev, Vitke points out that revolutions change policies and economics as well as *the entire culture.* In particular, the revolutionary crisis descends to the deepest strata of work cooperation to alter its style in a fundamental way. This is where it starts genuine creative transformation and reveals its potential new content.

Vitke cautioned that this strenuous work could take years and even decades. He also warned against underestimating the challenges involved. This difficult work of cultural transformation could be done only if the "zeal of emotional storm" is replaced with the true "zeal of routine work." He adds that doing this "hard cultural work" is certainly impossible "without the durable auger of scientific methodology", without *fully realizing the enormous value of scientific management for revolutionary transformation.*

What is this fundamental value of NOU? What does it mean to extend scientific principles to administration as an area of *social relations?*

Vitke answers in line with his concept of essential similarity between natural and social sciences. Indeed, certain objective laws apply to society as well as to nature. Since administration focuses primarily on social relations, NOU results from the invasion of science into social development. "Human machines are beginning to be built intentionally and consciously like mechanical machines before them."[6]

How feasible is this? Vitke's answer was a resolute "yes". He wrote that the individualistic spirit of industrial capitalism, its own practices notwithstanding, does not and cannot agree with this option because it automatically rejects social anarchy. The global social crisis, however, has already challenged mankind with the task of replacing the anarchic social system with a regulated one. The stability of the latter, Vitke maintains, depends not so much on its ability to regulate political or ideological movements but rather on that to "regulate the very fabric of social life, especially *work cooperation.*" Regrettably, he points out, so far we have learned to detect social laws only in major events of history. As for social laws of a microscopic scale that permeate everyday life, particularly work, only a tiny fraction of these laws has been discovered so far. Vitke's words refer primarily to the laws of design and operation of work collectives. These laws certainly exist, he wrote, and learning them will provide an opportunity to turn today's blind, spontaneous and largely chaotic common work into efficient cooperation by design. Psychology and sociology testify to the existence of these laws of molecular social processes at every step; moreover, they can be seen in everyday life even by the naked eye. Once these laws are discovered and understood, work collectives could be designed to function at a maximum efficiency as true social machines.

This idea, according to Vitke, reveals the true cultural and historical meaning of scientific administration. As he sums up, NOU "employs microscopic analysis, observation and

---

[6] See: Vitke N.A., Scientific Organization of Management Technology (Nauchnaya organizatsiya administrativnoy tekhniki) / The Beginning of NOT. Forgotten Discussions and Ideas that Never Came to Life. [U istokov NOT: Zabytye diskussii i nerealizovannye idei]. Leningrad, 1990, p. 166.

experiments to meet urgent practical needs of the organic stage of the revolution by designing the most rational business structures. Moreover, this work lays a solid foundation of special knowledge for the regulated rather than anarchic social system."[7]

Therefore, in contrast to many of his contemporaries who, following Taylor, gravitated towards a technocratic approach (notably Gastev and his school), Vitke, as later Mayo, insisted on the immense importance of *social research into management?* "First of all, we need to break up with crude object-oriented thinking," he wrote, emphasizing that much like a piece of broadcloth is not just an article but rather a reflection of certain relations, management is not merely documents, archives, accounting systems and certificates but primarily "a certain system of social labor relations that supersedes the operation of tools."[8] *This interpretation positively overcame the limitations of technological and functional management concepts prevailing at that time.*

We need to mention that Vitke and his followers did not deny the importance of functional analysis. Following Fayol, the prominent French management scholar, they also identified 5 principal functions of management, i.e., planning, organizing, commanding, coordinating and controlling. While paying due respect to this theory, however, they strongly opposed the epidemic of "diagram addiction" and the function cult in management theory and practice. Mayzels, for instance, noted that functions "exist and operate regardless of whether they are drawn on paper or not, whether they are included in a diagram as active, or not. In real life we see people who exercise functions rather than function as such. Any function reflected as a chart is fictitious. It is just a fetish that is immediately assumed to have arms, legs, eyes and other properties that it does not possess. It is also assumed to need an autonomous department that usually fails to cope with its tasks and gradually starts swelling, regardless of the fact that a

---

7 Ibid., p. 167.

8 Vitke N.A., Scientific Organization of Management. (Nauchnya organizatsiya upravleniya). In "Scientific Management" (Nauchnaya organizatsiya tekhniki upravleniya). Moscow, 1924, p. 14.

department next door at the very same agency is already taking partial care of this function."[9] Mayzels ardently points to the danger of a hyper functional approach that may fragment management and cause "the functionality disease", a serious malady of a management system.

While sharing many conclusions with the French scientific management school led by Fayol, Vitke went further in his analysis of the collective nature of labor. A work organization, he wrote, is hardly a sum of functional organs that forms the social organism of an enterprise. In contrast to this interpretation, he developed a **holistic approach** to management. "So far, - he noted, - every branch of management has been invariably interpreted as something isolated and self-contained, i.e., out of general context." This approach, however, deals with "separate shreds and fragments of management that block the entire horizon."[10] He rightfully believes this approach must be changed. Management needs to be understood "as an integral process... in which every part works for other parts in close association with them. Specific issues in management are not independent problems that add up to a simple arithmetic sum. They are united intrinsically rather than mechanically as parts and aspects of the integrated management process." [11]

It is hardly possible to underestimate the importance of this concept that has become the cornerstone of modern management theories.

Note that Vitke did not restrict the concept of "an integrated social organism" to manufacturing. Any collective unity, he wrote, that strives for certain goals and objectives is a "social organism", a collective labor organization. A trade union, a party, a school or a bank pursue a variety of goals, yet

---

[9] Mayzels R.S., Management and Organization of Agencies. (Upravlenie i organizatsiya uchrezhdeniy). P. 46.
[10] The First Moscow Initiative Conference on the Standardization of Management Methods. [*Pervaya Moskovskaya initsiativnaya konferentsiya po normalizatsii tekhniki upravleniya.*] September 21-23, 1922. Moscow, 1922. P.10.
[11] Ibid.

have something fundamental in common. All of them are "social machines" and "collective labor unions." The collective life of any of these machines results from the entire range of collective aspirations rather than the actions of a single person. The harmony between their parts does not emerge spontaneously and needs to be maintained by continuous organizational efforts. Accordingly, NOT has to move far beyond the borders of "manufacturing per se", a field to which it has largely been restricted. "NOT work must cover the entire field of collective labor and all collective labor machines where man cooperates or competes with man."[12]

It is significant that Vitke did not limit himself to a simple declaration of the need for a holistic approach, its methodological value notwithstanding. The organic integration of management, he wrote, is accomplished by means of a special **administrative** function that unites all the areas of management. Collective life and collective work need a degree of organization and harmony that, as noted above, cannot emerge spontaneously. The performance of a group is not a simple arithmetic sum of individual performances. A group of people inspired with the best of intentions but lacking an organizing center is anarchic and powerless. When man sets up a social union he must instill it with the same kind of purposeful harmony found in nature and reproduced in man-made machines.

Such a harmony is achieved precisely by means of the administrative function that "creates" a successful social life at an enterprise that is conducive to better performance. The significance and sophistication of this function increase with the number of workers and the complexity of the organization. Administration, Vitke continues, is a specific social activity that focuses on targeted influence on personnel to address issues such as the sound division of labor, stability of the organization, hiring and retaining personnel, labor incentives, sustained individual and collective interest in production, as

---

[12] Vitke N.A., Ecole d'Etudes Administratives in France. *(Frantsuzskaya shkola eksperimental'nogo administrirovaniya)* / The Beginning of NOT. P. 183.

well as good coordination among individuals and groups. These objectives are shared by any business organization.

Administrative functions must be performed in a continuous, methodical, planned and science-based fashion. This is "an imperative in our times of mass organizations and rigorous rationalism". They must also be based on scientific knowledge and meticulous experimental studies.

The need for a distinct administrative function is the core of Vitke's theories. He believes the significance of this function increases with the complexity of manufacturing, which requires a special group of *administrators*. "The modern administrator, - Vitke explains, - is largely a social technician or engineer (depending on his rank in the system), **a constructor of human relations.** The higher his office, the larger the number of subordinates he unites and guides, the larger is the proportion of administrative activities in his work vs. technological or engineering activities." [13] Indeed, this same idea was later confirmed by Elton Mayo during the Hawthorne studies.

Vitke clearly understood the diversity of management aspects and the importance of financial incentives. He gave full credit to American pioneers in this field who "incorporate a carefully designed pay scale into the new management system." At the same time, he continues, "*all of them, including Taylor himself, were slaves to the individualistic philosophy based on the concept of the isolated worker motivated solely by monetary interests.*" They did discover the stimulating effect of the differentiated wage system but failed to go any further.

Vitke believed there was much more to management than a good pay system. In this area the Russian scholar went considerably further than Taylor and even Fayol. First and foremost, Vitke had a deeper feeling of psychological aspects in collective labor. He argued that the essence of administration is not to develop production plans or introduce a system of financial incentives (which is certainly important) but to *create a favorable social and psychological atmosphere in labor*

---

[13] Vitke N.A., Organization of Management and Industrial Development. P. 72.

collectives, to cultivate the so-called "spirit of the hive". "No precise planning of the production process, nor an ideal regulation of responsibilities, or the best mechanical control of the manufacturing flow can make an efficient organization, - he wrote. - The automatism of social labor cannot be fostered against people's will, or even in the absence of such will: A system thus created would be lifeless."[14]

The main goal of day-to-day administrative efforts is to create this atmosphere of friendly mass cooperation. It is a great and fine art to combine the universally acknowledged business and moral *authority* of the administrator with the broadest grassroots *initiative* possible.

Vitke expands on this thought. It is not nearly enough to divide an organization into proper structural units, draft dozens of paper instructions and regulations, man all desks or machines (even with well selected personnel) and provide a minimum of amenities to workers. These are little more than *prerequisites* of good collective cooperation that has yet to be generated and sustained. A social machine thus designed must be inspired with a "live soul" of ownership and work enthusiasm.

Vitke's methodological concept of a leader as primarily a social engineer, a "constructor of human relations" was a constructive starting point for research into an important area such as *methods and style* of management. On the basis of this concept he formulated a number of deep thoughts on the logics of leadership, ethics of relations with subordinates, and so on.

The scholar believes that a manager must be predominantly *a social leader* rather than an outstanding engineer. He need not be an expert in various work processes or a tough supervisor of the old-type authoritarian organization. He also needs not be an expert in advance planning, calculations, training or quality control. "All these functions are already delegated to a complex automated work collective."

---

[14] Ibid., p. 77.

While the administrator should be fully aware of operational and technological situation, he has no need to deal with them directly. He is mostly a social engineer whose goal is to unite and coordinate the efforts of partial technicians, select appropriate personnel for his staff and the like. With the help of this staff, he works hard to find appropriate human resources, educate workers, and unite them into a harmonious whole. He is to charge everybody with a clear-cut area of responsibility, set objectives for every team and provide directives, continuously coordinate the work of various departments and carefully control the execution of his orders.

The administrator's main risk, Vitke wrote, is to "succumb to the prejudiced mentality of the isolated worker, a self-proclaimed know-all who scatters his energy over thousands of petty technical problems involved in a function or a job to be done. The administrator must feel like a ship captain who directs his vessel and controls its progress. His greatest concern is to avoid believing that he is the best expert in any field. It is his right and duty, for instance, to give orders to the engine room concerning the speed of the ship, control performance and conduct inspections. His visit to the engine room to teach the mechanic how to handle the boiler, however, would be counterproductive. An idea that the administrator should or has the right to personally instruct the worker on technical aspects of his job is probably the worst legacy of the vanishing era of authoritarian management."

This mentality, Vitke argues, is a thing of the past. Now the task is "to kindle team spirit, foster collective enthusiasm and understanding of work, achieve conscious coordination among numerous people, evoke collective energy and drive the steam engine of the organization along the track of manufacturing regulations."

Selection and retention of personnel was an issue of critical importance to Vitke. He wrote that the best drawing is useless if a machine or a house is built from an inferior material. The result would be a cheap imitation of a watch instead of a chronometer. Likewise, no seven-story house can be built from dried clay rather than firebrick. Social engineering in this sense does not differ much from industrial engineering. A strong structure needs good human material.

We should learn how to build sturdy structures, not flimsy wooden cabins.

Using whatever is at hand in a hope of "replacing" it by something better in the future is not a good habit. Can a machine work properly if its parts are replaced every day? Certainly not. Individual parts are not as important as the harmony of the whole mechanism. A machine tool is appreciated exactly because of this harmony that cannot be created overnight even by the most experienced engineer. Old violins have a great value, but an association of people is even more sophisticated than a musical instrument. Carnegie was right when he said that he would need a generation to restore the organization of his factories. The administrator must give up the bad habit of individualistic thinking when he does not see the forest for the trees, i.e., sees individual Ivanovs and Petrovs rather than that intangible factor that "unites all Ivanovs and Petrovs in a harmonious *social organization.*"

Vitke portrayed a clear image of a leader as a "social engineer" who professes *democratic management*, can unite all team members with common aspirations and evoke their initiative and creativity. To this end, he should be vigorous, charismatic and well-organized. He should also learn how to adjust his habits when needed, control his will and his attitudes, know his duties, and make people respect his authority. He should also demand strict organization from his subordinates and at the same time, be always available for consultations.

While opposing the democratic style of management to a bureaucratic one, Vitke repeatedly noted that the main difference between the two is *the respectful attitude to subordinates,* regrettably, many administrators still ignore this requirement. Their unsolicited insults and rudeness explained by the ostensible need for discipline make workers bitter and unhappy. Unfair treatment increases personnel turnover and certainly does not help improve performance. A manager's talent is no excuse for insolence. The human factor may be efficiently activated only when the manager respects the dignity of others, spares their feelings and encourages workers to take full advantage of their potential.

This train of thought is of enormous importance. We see again how the Russian author challenges the classic school that focused on the organizational and technical aspects of management while largely ignoring its social essence. Vitke asserted that a powerful manager is anything but a technician, even an outstanding one. Above all he must be "the *leader* of a human collective".

The increasing significance of the administrative function, he believes, warrants establishing a true **administration science, an integrated system of knowledge** about "the rational design and management of labor collectives in an industrial society."[15] Vitke emphasized more than once that this science concerns *human cooperation* and *associated labor organizations* rather than just work.

Vitke did not overestimate the modest progress made in the establishment of this discipline which he calls NOU, "administrative technology" or "social engineering". "It has barely emerged. No large edifice has been built yet, just a few isolated structures and a heap of bricks are available."[16] As to whether the new discipline should be a theoretical or purely an applied science, Vitke also provided some insights into this problem. He realized the inadequacy of a purely theoretical approach when "generalizations become a self-contained objective" and live links to actual practices are lost. He thought, however, that excessive pragmatism, when any improvement in work techniques is labeled as a product of "scientific management" is another extreme, since it often hides a lack of care for research.[17]

Both deviations, as Vitke correctly maintains, are harmful. "Success in any area of technology... needs an intimate connection between theory and practice, their mutual diffusion and enough room for each of these intertwining lines

---

[15] Ibid., p. 132.
[16] Vitke N.A., Issues in Management. In "Issues of Organization and Management" *(Voprosy organizatsii i upravleniya)*, 1922, No.2. P. 21.
[17] Vitke N.A., Organization of Management and Industrial Development. P. 8.

to develop."[18] Cutting off either of these lines would inevitably slow down progress as a whole and distorts its direction. It would be hard to find better words.

Unfortunately, Vitke argued, Soviet NOT had progressed in precisely such a slow and distorted way. In fact, he did not think too high of Russian NOT achievements after the October revolution. Leaving aside certain exciting and symptomatic pre-revolutionary efforts, NOT during the revolutionary period, he wrote, was largely *isolated from the practice it was meant to serve and improve.*

NOT's "yesterday" involved no broad applied movement. Industrial practice during that period did not care for any scientific (or even elementary) improvements and therefore ignored scientific management.

This does not mean that NOT's "yesterday" was theoretical or, as they say now, "academic", he continues. The situation in this area was not ideal either. "NOT in Russia could hardly engage in meaningful original research since it was lacking a practical base. Indeed, theoretical output in this area has been patchy and insignificant."[19] In other words, NOT in post-revolutionary Russia, according to Vitke, was inadequate in terms of theory and isolated from practical life as well. Therefore, Russian NOT could only be called an ideological discipline. [20]

Vitke called for dramatic changes in Russian NOT and suggested Henri Fayol's school of experimental administration as an excellent model.[21]

---

[18] Vitke N.A., Organizational issues in today's NOT. (Organizatsionnye voprosy sovremennogo NOT). Scientific Management. P.22.

[19] Vitke N.A., Organization of Management and Industrial Development. *(Organizatsiya upravleniya i industrialnoe razvitie.)* Moscow, 1925. P. 156.

[20] We should add that, despite Vitke's hopes and forecasts, NOT in Russia remained purely ideological until the collapse of the Soviet regime.

[21] Vitke's paper on this school (Ecole d'ètudes administrative) is included in this book.

Chapter 2. Prominent Supporters of the New Trend[22]

1. I.S. Kanegisser

Ioakim S. Kanegisser, one of the brightest representatives of the Russian social organization school in management, was an engineer and an industrial manager well-known even before the 1917 revolution. In 1899 he became chief manager of a major Russian factory. On his initiative, industrial management courses were added to the curriculum of several Petersburg engineering schools after 1917; some lectures were read by Kanegisser himself.

Kanegisser's publications reveal that he was skeptical about the Bolshevik revolution and the subsequent policy of "war Communism". He believed that if the new system relied solely on the "new mentality," it could hardly be productive. No person could be motivated to work exclusively by the call of duty. The principal, though not the only one, motivation of zealous work is the personal monetary interest. "This was the case under capitalism, - he said from the podium of the First All-Russian NOT conference, - and it will continue under socialism or communism. To be productive, a worker must directly benefit from his efforts ..."[23]

Kanegisser was among those participants in the conference who strongly opposed anti-Taylorist presentation by Academicians Bekhterev and Yermanskiy but correctly

---

[22] Much of this chapter relies on our earlier joint publications with Prof. E.B. Koritskiy. See Koritskiy E.B., Nintsieva G.V. and Shcherbakovskiy G.Z. Nascent, Scientific Management: a Historical Tour of Russian and Global Management Thought. Book 2. Frankfurt-am-Main, 2007, pp. 41-57.

[23] Kanegisser I.S., Pay Systems and Their Application. Proceedings of the First All-Russian Initiating NOT Conference. *[Sistemy oplaty truda i praktika ikh primeneniya. Trudy Pervoy Vserossiyskoy initsiativnoy konferentsii...]*. Volume 4. Moscow, 1921. P. 35.

noted that Taylor's system, for all its specific flaws, was an outstanding achievement of human thought that had seriously improved the entire production mechanism of the capitalist society.

Kanegisser described his own vision of scientific management and administration in a fundamental three-volume book that ranks among the best works of that period.[24]

He understood the organization of an enterprise as a selection of forces, means and measures which in their entirety ensure the execution of all the necessary actions and operations.

Any enterprise should aim at maximum productivity of labor. This, however, requires full coordination between all the elements of production, i.e., plant (structures, equipment and materials) and human elements (workers, office staff and engineers). In addition to these tangible elements there is also a most important factor such as *time.*

Kanegisser identified three possible types of organization:

1. traditional (non-systematic) organization,

2. systematic organization,

3. scientific organization.

The scholar meticulously analyzed each of these types of organization that exist in actual economic life.

In non-systematic organization, management is dominated by subjective factors. Each and every new problem is addressed as a matter of personal discretion that often depends on one's disposition or intuition. The success of the business almost entirely depends on the abilities, memory and management skills of individual executives. Unfortunately,

---

[24]See: Kanegisser I.S., Administration in the Metal-Working Industry: A Manual. *[Prakticheskoe rukovodstvo po administrativno-hozyaistvennoi organizatsii proizvodstvennykh predpriyatiy, v chastnosti, metalloobrabatyvayushchikh.]* Parts 1-3. Petersburg, 1923-1924.

wrote Kanegisser, this non-systematic organization prevails at the vast majority of Russian enterprises.[25]

Systematic organization aims at a better use of time and careful attitude to machinery. It implies better control over production due to enhanced reporting. During the evolution of systematic organization several rules of thumb were formulated based on common sense. They are as follows:

1) The master action plan must be designed with utmost care so as to cover all the actions needed and include nothing unnecessary;

2) All the planned actions must follow a certain schedule that rules out any loss of time;

3) Work must be distributed among all the participants to be completed as soon as possible;

4) To save time, any issues related to various departments or various persons in one department should be addressed by discussing them at meetings with the parties concerned; membership in panels discussing various types of issues should be defined precisely;

5) Executive functions of individuals should be separated well enough to avoid any conflict and waste of time;

6) Duties must be allocated in such a way that instructions or orders concerning one problem would be issued to an employee by only one person;

7) Candidates should be hired to perform a certain function; there should be no idle employees for whom functions have to be invented;

8) Every employee should spend all his time on work; valuable workers should not perform jobs that can be done by someone with fewer skills;

9) Since any job can be performed faster if it is monotonous and routine, division of labor must be applied as much as possible;

---

[25]Ibid., part 1. P. 13.

10) Certain conditions must be established for any task;

11) Raw materials must meet appropriate standards and consumed in accordance with the actual need;

12) If the previous rule has to be waived to save time, it must be done according to a precise calculation;

13) Purchases of materials and tools must be preceded by careful research into quality and prices and made well in advance to receive them at the time needed;

14) Tools and materials must be stored properly, accessed and transported easily; data on their movement should be readily available to all whom it may concern;

15) Tools must be kept in good order to extend their service life and prevent delays caused by malfunctioning;

16) Orders should be taken on the basis of cost and time calculations in the context of the master plan and action program for the factory;

17) Execution of tasks should be continuously monitored to prevent omissions that may cause delays;

18) The work process should be managed in such a way that it would not suffer from erroneous orders;

19) Remuneration should fully depend on productivity;

20) Work environment must meet sanitary and hygienic requirements not only because of humane considerations, but also to ensure that workers are in good health to perform their regular duties.

Kanegisser correctly notes that the emergence and progress of systematic organization was a major step forward. However, this type of organization also has its flaws because many of its management techniques are based on supervision and compulsion rather than objective factors. The system is still centered on personal qualities of the boss, his abilities, attitudes, management style and character. In many cases a change of the leader shattered the entire management system at an enterprise. In other words, systematic organization makes but a partial contribution to reaching the main objective of any business, i.e., maximum productivity (producing the maximum amount of goods at a minimum cost over a certain period of time).[26]

Therefore, Kanegisser observed, the emergence of *scientific* organization and its practical application in the economy appeared highly natural. He believed that the main feature of scientific management is that each and every element of work is investigated by means of observation whose results are meticulously recorded, studied and compared to produce certain rules, laws and formulas. Accordingly, scientific organization is based on solid principles.

Principle 1. Any managerial action must be based on scientific data. Any decision must rely upon an investigation of all factors that have an effect on the process to be controlled.

Principle 2. Scientific selection of equipment, materials and workers, i.e., the physical and human factors of production. Personnel selection that takes into account workers' abilities and fitness for a specific position is especially critical.

Principle 3. Continuous training. Under the non-systematic and even systematic organization the techniques for performing a particular job were determined by workers themselves. Scientific organization, on the other hand, requires specialists to review all possible options, choose the best one in terms of time and energy savings, and teach workers how to use it.

Principle 4. New relations between managers and workers. The manager increasingly turns from a supervisor to a helping boss who serves his workers and prepares whatever is necessary for the actual work of his subordinates.[27]

The application of these four principles in practice requires certain steps. For instance, all jobs must be split down into the simplest elements subject to painstaking scientific analysis. The worker must be genuinely interested in the outcome of his work. "Every worker should know that an increase in his productivity would lead to an increase in his bonus, not the work quota... [Under the old systems] if a

---

[26]Ibid., p. 19.
[27]Ibid., p. 27.

worker makes more than the management considers normal at the given piece rate, next time the piece rate would drop. In this situation it makes little sense to the worker to increase productivity; he would rather *pretend* to be doing his best. Conversely, under the scientific system it is known precisely how long each job should last, and the standard piece rate is established once and for all (if the work technique does not change). Therefore, the worker benefits from an increased output by getting paid the highest bonus."[28]

Kanegisser stressed, however, that these policies alone are not sufficient. Like Vitke, he believed that industrial management is based on governing human collectives, and its most important component is the **social** aspect. Of special interest are his thoughts on the work style and qualities of a manager.

The most distinct feature of management is its impact on people. "The most perfect plant and the most perfect organizational scheme at a factory remain dead in the absence of people to operate machines and perform according to the scheme; only people invigorate any business and any factory. Good management means making people act right."[29] One of the critical challenges faced by any manager is to sustain a physical and moral environment that satisfies rather than oppresses the workers. Strict discipline is certainly mandatory to maintain order and achieve success; all policies established at a factory must be rigorously followed. Yet even the strictest of disciplines does not mean that the manager should not be polite with his subordinates. Even a harsh reprimand should not be rude, since "rudeness annoys people, insults their self-respect and reduces their zeal at work."[30] Likewise, the manager should never make fun of his subordinates. "On the one hand, it makes people bitter, on the other hand, gives them a right to familiarities which undermine the manager's authority."[31]

---

[28]Ibid., P. 94.
[29]Ibid., p. 95.
[30]Ibid.
[31]Ibid.

Kanegisser formulated a rule that should be kept in mind by all current as well as future managers. "Composure and respectful criticism are way more effective than persistent shouting and swearing that many consider an indispensable attribute of power."[32]

Another insightful observation by the author that will hold for the foreseeable future is that a manager should have no "pets". In any conflict between employees the manager's decision must make an impartial decision and enforce it consistently. Only justice can build up trust from subordinates, whereas workers who see a weakness for "pets" develop an aversion to the manager himself and the business he is in charge of.

Kanegisser writes with indignation about managers who encourage or even just put up with the system of reporting on colleagues, spying and mutual surveillance that supposedly prevent abuses and help keep workers under tight control. This is a dangerous delusion. Such a system only sows mutual distrust and certainly does not help teamwork. Something fundamentally different is needed. The manager must foster an atmosphere where abuses are impossible or promptly discovered; if someone feels hurt or sees a colleague's mistake, he should speak up. Transparency must prevail at work. If everybody knows that "an honest complaint will cause no repressions from anybody, and the matter will always be addressed impartially, no one will be afraid to openly note any mistakes, while the manager's awareness will be enhanced."[33]

Kanegisser always insisted that a manager must be a social leader. While demanding order and discipline from his subordinates, he must ensure that their life and work environment met their physical and moral needs. He especially valued the factor of "confidence and stability of employment", since with high personnel turnover "work cannot be concerted and productive."

As he was discussing an issue of career growth, promotions and so on, Kanegisser expanded on his thoughts

---

[32]Ibid.
[33]Ibid.

about the inadmissibility of "pets". "Promotions must be granted only to worthy workers with true merits who are also fit for a higher position. No other reasons justify a promotion. Any favoritism causes jealousy, frustration and loss of enthusiasm in those who feel left out."[34] One can hardly argue with this observation.

Kanegisser also believed that any leader should skillfully combine monetary and psychological leverage. He tirelessly emphasized the importance of moral, psychologically sound and ethically weighed factors that are much more efficient than "incessant bothering, bossing around, reprimands and harassment." On the other hand, moral factors alone are not enough to "continuously foster perseverance and diligence." They should be complemented with financial incentives, so that "any increase in individual productivity that benefits the enterprise would also result in a higher pay for the worker."

Kanegisser believed that the traditional pay increases with seniority were a reasonable practice, since any worker accumulates knowledge and experience with time. Moreover, they are a good way to retain personnel. Nevertheless, he held that such increases should be granted on a case-by-case basis rather than automatically. He made a truly sound point (that, unfortunately, has yet to gain a wide recognition) by stating that pay should be determined "not by seniority but only by the benefits that the business receives from the worker."[35] In other words, he was essentially saying that salaries should be based on the ultimate results of one's work. As for seniority, according to Kanegisser it should be remunerated by special bonuses (either on a periodic basis or as severance pay) that progressively increase with the number of years spent at the enterprise.

He also identified a number of indispensable managerial qualities particularly applicable to factory directors. Note that his theoretical conclusions were largely based on priceless own experience. What are these qualities?

---

[34]Ibid.
[35]Ibid.

Kanegisser held that a director must be a person of forceful character, strong will and firm values; he should clearly understand his wishes and aspirations so that "everyone at the factory feels it." His instructions "must be precise and certain."[36]

It is critical that a senior manager has "an agile mind" and a good reaction in order to promptly deal with issues, since a fast decision is sometimes more valuable than the ideal option taking a long time to find. In actual industrial situations, to quote Peter the Great's ditto, "delays are often fatal." Even if such a manager makes one mistake in ten cases, it would still be better than making ten correct decisions after lengthy deliberations.

Kannegisser admits that some strategic problems require careful and time-consuming research. It is at least thoughtless to address them without a collective discussion. Many current factory problems, however, need prompt attention.

A good manager should know how to admit his mistakes without feeling embarrassed. Any attempt to blame others because of false pride would undermine his authority much more than the mistake itself.

A good manager must be capable of selecting personnel to meet specific job requirements, clearly allocate responsibilities among workers and coordinate their actions.

He should also have a deep knowledge of his factory. If its activities are diverse, Kanegisser writes, the director certainly cannot and should not be an expert on all of them. Moreover, this will give him a chance to avoid typical flaws such as subjectivism and micromanagement. However, he does need general engineering expertise in the given industry and a broad-minded attitude, "lest it become difficult to monitor the business and make judgments on its progress."[37] He need not feel shy if his subordinates have better expertise in a specific

---

[36]Ibid., p. 80.
[37]Ibid., p. 81.

area. Rather, he should use the chance to listen to and maybe even learn something from his staff.

Other valuable qualities of a good director include common sense, self-confidence and a talent to instill trust in employees, which "sustains their good spirits and courage in dire straits."

Absolute honesty and credibility are also indispensable. "Where the boss's honesty is in doubt, his subordinates will never be loyal to the business."[38] When combined with resolve, cordiality and benevolence, honesty guarantees undisputable authority to the director.

The director of a factory has a wide range of responsibilities. At any given moment he must be aware of the situation throughout the business.

For instance, he should always know the financial position of the factory and make sure necessary funds are available. He must also secure profitable contracts and monitor their timely and high-quality delivery. He must have full knowledge of the behavior and activities of his workers, as well as their needs. Finally, he must continuously improve organization and management at the enterprise.

It is not easy for the director of a large business to cope with these numerous and variegated duties. If he were willing (as many in fact are trying) to look into every detail and personally manage all the tiny aspects of the business, he would have no time to deal with strategic issues such as management improvement, business development, studies into related industries and so on and so forth.

According to Kanegisser, this major problem can be addressed by delegating the authority to deal with most current issues to carefully selected and trusted personnel. At the same time, each department must submit regular reports that would give the director an opportunity "to be aware of everything at the factory without leaving his office."[39]

---

[38]Ibid., p. 95.
[39]Ulitskiy Ya.S., The Logic of Management. An essay on the theory of management in administrative collectives. *[Logika*

The above-said provides clear evidence of the valuable contribution made by I.S.Kanegisser to the social school of scientific management in Russia.

2. Ya.S. Ulitskiy

Yakov Ulitskiy was another remarkable supporter of the social approach in management theory. He focused on investigating managerial work by identifying its individual components to find out certain regular elements, "the basic laws of good management."[40]

Western economists spent serious efforts on investigating a capitalist manager as the organizer of a large economic agent. For instance, Schumpeter created a romantic image of a manager as an economic leader, an "industrial captain" who unites capital, goods and people on a tremendous scale. Ulitskiy believed it was high time for Russian economists to focus on the issue of managers and work out "a schematic image of a manager of a state-owned enterprise."[41] Economic practice and life itself did require this kind of work since they were in dire need of new organizational forces. A similar suggestion came from S.D. Strelbitskiy, another outstanding representative of the Russian social school in management (see next paragraph) who noted that without science it would be impossible to overcome routine management patterns "...that have probably made little progress since the time of Egyptian pyramid builders."[42]

Using the same language as Vitke, Ulitskiy wrote that it was hard to overestimate the role of leadership in the management system whose success largely depends on his

---

upravleniya. Ocherk po teorii upravleniya administrativnymi kollektivami.] Kiev, 1924. P. 82.
[40] Ibid.
[41] Ibid.
[42] Strelbitskiy S.D., The Administrator [Administrator]. Kharkov, 1923. P. 6.

abilities, skills, experience and the talent to evoke energy and enthusiasm in the entire collective. The manager is "a social engineer" who organizes and governs human masses. He must "convince everybody that their business is important and communicate energy and enthusiasm to a complex human machine. He must align all the disjointed actions of this machine. His task is that of social construction."[43]

Ulitskiy maintained that managers in any area, be it a factory, a cooperative or a university, share several features that do not belong to the area of technology and apply to any collective. It is these qualities that are covered by the scientific management theory.[44]

Ulitskiy's thoughts on the theory of management are of considerable interest. He compared this discipline to logic, a science that determines whether the process of thinking is correct or erroneous. The tasks of logic are

1) To establish rules under which the process of thinking is good for expanding our knowledge;

2) Explain these rules by the laws of thinking;

3) Use these rules to identify and explain all the actual errors in thinking.[45]

Ulitskiy makes a significant comment on the above tasks of logic. One should not believe, he warns, that logic deals with rules that lead to the discovery of new truths. New ideas emerge regardless of the laws of thinking, due to *personal talents* that cannot be replaced by any rules and operate in unique ways that may seem a mystery to another individual in the same situation. *"A talented person makes brilliant discoveries or serendipitous guesses in situations where a common person without a creative spirit would not arrive at any guess even he knows as much as the former person. Therefore today's logic is the science of verification rather than discoveries."*[46]

---

[43] Ulitskiy Ya.S., The Logic of Management. P. 13.
[44] Ibid., p. 11.
[45] Ibid., p.14.
[46] Ibid.

Likewise, he thought that the theory of management was similar to logic as applied to administration, the science of "right and wrong methods in management." The theory of management explores the rules and conditions that ensure a maximum output at a minimum cost.

Many people think in the right way but have no clue to logic as a science. In a similar way, many excellent administrators in charge of major institutions may have never studied the theory of management. Ulitskiy occasionally put too much emphasis on the importance of managerial "intuition" or "talent". Nevertheless, it is hard to disagree with his observation that "much like a person intrinsically incapable of logical thinking cannot learn it with the help of logic, a "bad" administrator that has no talent cannot become a "good" one by studying the theory of management – that, incidentally, would be indispensable to a "good" administrator with **an innate gift for management**.[47]

What are the features of this administrative talent? The **first one** is *a capacity for abstract and theoretical thinking.* This, as Ulitskiy put it, does not mean a manager should be "a classical theoretician". There is no distinct border between scientific research and daily functioning of the brain, in both cases the process of thinking includes the same components such as observation, comparison, identification of similarities, elaboration of general patterns and so on. While studying reports and papers as symbols of real facts and actions in his office, an administrator gets used to employing certain formulas; all specific facts reach him in an abstract and summarized form. Therefore he can grasp large and complex strata of reality only with the use of theoretical thinking. Otherwise the manager would just "drown" in countless details and see "just a little corner of the entire picture."[48]

The second salient feature of the administrative talent is *the feeling of live reality.* It is critical that a manager never lose the connection between isolated symbols (figures, reports diagrams and the like) and the reality behind them. Whenever

---

[47] Ibid.
[48] Ibid., p. 17-19.

reading figures or reports he should always conduct reality checks. Bureaucratic degeneration, according to Ulitskiy, consists exactly in the loss of connection between paper symbols and their specific living content. "A certain kind of duality starts in this case; the facts of life are linked in one order, while their images (papers) talk about some entirely different relations."[49]

The third critical component of the administrative talent is a gift Ulitskiy calls *the spirit of calculation.* Whether consciously or not, a good administrator has a command of accounting and statistics. He subliminally differentiates between significant and trivial indicators, classifies them according to similar qualities and so on.[50]

According to Ulitskiy, therefore, management is primarily an art that can be mastered only by people with an appropriate talent. He certainly conceded that laws and principles of management to be studied by administrators must be subject to scientific exploration. However, it is simply impossible to develop specific managerial instructions for each specific case. Management is a creative process that has many individual aspects depending on the administrator's personality.

He concludes that *the theory of management should establish organizational principles that apply to any collective entity and help issue administrative orders and identify inappropriate actions.* The theory of management in this sense serves as an "education" for managers that can occasionally even substitute for genuine talent. *Yet a gift for management, according to Ulitskiy, prevails over any "education."*[51]

Ulitskiy, therefore, believed that management *was science and an art at one and the same time,* though art obviously had a priority. This view is at least debatable, since it comes dangerously close to allowing discretionary management. However, we should credit Ulitskiy with initiating a discussion of an important methodological issue.

------

[49] Ibid., p. 19.
[50] Ibid., p. 24.
[51] Ibid., p. 63-64.

3. S.D. Strelbitskiy

Strelbitskiy, another notable adept of the social school, had a somewhat different view. He believed that management should not be regarded exclusively as an art that could be mastered only by naturally gifted people. The role of talent could certainly not be denied. To an even greater extent, however, management is a science exploring its own laws. As any other science, it rests on profound investigations into the economy, particularly industry, and experiments without which "intellectual power would be dispersed in futile deliberation." Russian reforms are in dire need of a theory of management. However, no fast results should be expected here since we are talking of a long and painstaking process rather than a one-time event. In the meanwhile, administration remains largely an art; only the discovery of objective laws will turn it into a genuine science.

Strelbitskiy developed a meaningful concept of management. Let us consider his basic points.

He understood industrial management as primarily the management of human collectives. Management or administration (he believed these terms were essentially interchangeable) is "the process of organizing the human thought and directing it towards a certain goal," Strelbitskiy S.D. The Administrator [Administrator]. Kharkov, 1923. P. 6.

I.e., the achievement of the planned result of work in the shortest time possible that would be "closest to the ideal time mathematically calculated with the help of special experiments." Ibid., p. 8.

The cornerstone of Strelbitskiy's concepts was time as a criterion that justified (or not justified) the existence of any production unit. Scientific management, he believed, is based on precise calculations aimed at saving time.

A manager striving for the ideal duration of production processes must always keep in mind that to be as short as possible, such a process must be linear, i.e., the article should follow a straight line from the raw materials warehouse to the finished product storage. The shorter this line, the less time is needed for manufacturing. Ideally, it should go straight from the starting point to the end point. This line should be studied in a scientific way by the administrator: (1) Receipt of raw material from the warehouse, (2) Delivery to the first machine tool; (3) Processing by the first machine tool; (4) Delivery to the second machine tool; (5) Processing by the second machine tool; (6) Delivery to the third machine tool; (7) Processing by the third machine tool; (8) Delivery to the warehouse; (9) Acceptance of the product by the warehouse. For the sake of simplification Strelbitskiy deliberately omits "segments" such as acceptance of raw materials at the first warehouse; release of the finished product from the second warehouse and so on. To find the "ideal" time needed to manufacture the product under the best conditions, we should precisely measure the time spent on passing each segment and sum up the results. For the purposes of this exercise the best tools, transportation facilities and workforce should be supplied in advance to each of these segments; also, any excuse for downtime such as the lack of raw materials should be eliminated. See Ibid., p. 9.

The result, however, can be called "ideal" only as a rough approximation. Each segment may be further divided into even smaller sections up to the very "primary elements" (individual operations and motions). Only a study of these primary elements can lead to the precise "ideal" time to within split seconds. With the right methodology, this time would probably differ from the actual time in real production by an order of magnitude or even more due to rest periods, various other breaks (needed as well as unneeded) and a number of other factors that in their entirety "slacken the pace" of work.

Since a key objective of any manager is to sustain a high speed of production, any slackening should be regarded as a major malfunction at any enterprise. Usually, it is caused by deviations from the "linearity" of the production process. The most graphic example is the "return movement" when an article goes back from machine tool #2 to machine tool #1. Even more often the article would be returned from some machine #10 to the warehouse and wait to be sent to machine #11. In such cases, the straight production line turns into a "star-like zigzag", with the slackening directly proportional to the number of "rays". Some other unfortunate factors in the industry do not violate the straight production line principle but also slow down the process. These bottlenecks (or "blank spots, as Strelbitskiy called them) emerge when the throughput at one of the segments is for some reason lower than at the previous or the next segment. This leads to jams, downtime and eventually a drop in production speed.

A manager would secure a time gain only if he makes the production process as straightforward as possible. However, this principle alone is not the only condition of success. Another critical component of time savings is the principle of "parallel operations" or "compacting". Ibid., p. 12.

The production process usually consists of a number of "parallel straight lines" that should be well coordinated. "If one parallel process operates faster than the other, its output is sent to the warehouse to be used when needed; in this case we encounter a typical "return movement" that slows down production, to say nothing of economic losses caused by surplus inventory accumulation. If a parallel process lags behind, the "node" would contain what we have agreed to call a blank spot." Ibid.

Major enterprises usually feature a dense network of parallel production lines plus several subsidiary work lines. The manager must "equalize work speed along all these lines to eliminate "blank spots", "return movements" and other flaws". In other words, he should "command the factory" and have a picture of it that would be "clear as daylight". The graphic method can be of use in reaching this goal. Lines and figures in a correctly drawn diagram literally "speak up", so things overlooked or seemingly trivial reveal their true significance. Strelbitskiy recommended every factory manager to have a schematic representation of production lines that would indicate the "ideal" time calculated experimentally for each segment of each straight line.

While giving due credit to material factors of production, Strelbitskiy still believed that good workers (the personal factor of production) are more critical for time-saving. He divided factory personnel into four groups as follows.

Group one: Workers directly dealing with manufacturing.

Group two: Workers whose efforts do not change the product they handle (e.g., transportation workers).

Group three: Managers and supervisors (administration, engineers, and technicians).

Group four: Clerks (accountants, time-keepers, and others).

It is critical for the factory manager to undertake a careful study into the need for workers from each group. Managers must bear in mind that "every redundant worker, even with a top performance, causes just as much harm to production speed as a vacant position of a missing worker." Ibid., p. 17.

Therefore the graphic representation of the production process with "ideal" times should certainly be complemented with figures concerning the "ideal" number of workers. A specific task of factory managers is to identify the soundest production lines based on the "straight line" and "parallelism" principles and to determine the precise number of skilled workers needed in each of the four groups.

Strelbitskiy had intriguing thoughts about leadership style, especially in the case of new managers. "On the one hand, the new manager feels a great responsibility, a lack of self-confidence and a fear that his first steps would be wrong; on the other hand, he is exposed to a kaleidoscope of machines, people, figures, and facts... All this falls upon the newcomer and makes him feel dizzy. It takes quite some time to identify the principal outline of the business and the value of each worker." Ibid., p. 23.

Strelbitskiy recommended that a new manager who wants to get an introduction to the factory should start at his office. "In order to deeply study a business, - he wrote, - one should have an idea of its basics and separate its framework from the details. This can well be done by listening to explanations and sketching diagrams of relations among departments and the administrative structure. Also, cash flow and financing needs are all the figures necessary to find out the status of available cash, warehouses, and the order portfolio and so on.

By careful questioning (making people speak is always better than speaking yourself) and declining any effort to burden you with details, you will also come to know the executives working at the factory. Only after learning about the business at the office and getting a clear idea of the entire facility you will be able to finish the first stage of your work by an actual tour of the factory as a master rather than a client. Indeed, once you know and see a graphic representation of the factory you will be able to plan yourself to get an integral impression of various departments." Ibid., p. 23-24.

The reverse order of familiarization that starts with a tour is just a loss of time, Strelbitskiy says, since in this case "you would just helplessly trail behind your escort, draw their attention to trivial details, listen to their explanations concerning some machine tools without any clue to the organizational structure of the business." Ibid., p. 24.

The second stage involves dynamic studies of the enterprise. After the initial exploration, the business is already visualized by the new manager as a clear array of functional departments and production lines rather than an obscure heap of workers, machines, and structures. At the next step, he should study how coordinated and commensurate they are. It is important not only to explore the actual business but also personnel, especially senior executives and their fitness for the job. Strelbitskiy alerted against going to extremes during this exercise. On the one hand, liberalism and hesitation are out of the question. "A person not suitable for the job should be fired. On the other hand, making personnel changes on a first impression can be even more harmful. First, there is always a risk of firing a fairly good worker. Moreover, summary dismissals may damage morale among other workers and in the collective as a whole." Ibid., p. 25.

Strelbitskiy also identified the following objective laws (principles) of managerial style that would apply to any field:

1. Much like the production process itself, the manager's thinking must be consistent and straightforward.

2. The manager's instructions should be resolute.

41

3. Personal management of a team must be rooted in the collective itself.

4. Every worker should be aware of his contribution to the common cause. Ibid., p. 27-28.

He elaborated on the first principle by noting that every stage in the production process must have a logical justification. Distinct, clear and consistent thoughts can appropriately materialize in the production process. "A good administrator issues precise instructions whose consequences for the process are already anticipated."

The second principle is a logical continuation of the first one. Determination is an integral part of any managerial decision. Orders given by the manager should be resolute, concise and yet exhaustive. The tone of an order makes a major difference, Strelbitskiy noted. A calm order by a resolute supervisor without exasperation has more chances to be precisely followed. He adds that "this elementary law of management, unfortunately, is too often violated... it is a pity to see an administrator who ruins his own efforts by being nervous and fussy."

The third component of scientific management is the principle of consultation and single authority. Strelbitskiy warned against excessive consultations as well as against abusing the single authority principle that should not mean "doing whatever pleases me." Ibid., p. 29.

In this context, the scholar referred to the good practice in the USA where factory directors convene senior executives (including department heads) to a daily one-hour meeting where work progress reports are usually presented by departments. This practice keeps all department heads informed of the general situation at the enterprise. Unfortunately, he wrote, these morning meetings had not yet become common in Russia.

He also recommended conducting meetings with specific workers and managers from various areas of the business.

Style is critical to these meetings. For instance, it makes utter sense for the manager to present an initiative he had already worked on as an ad hoc suggestion and prompt a discussion. He can thus check his assumptions and amend them without any impact on his authority, which would be inevitable if he just issued an inconsiderate order.

The fourth principle is associated with the previous one. Strelbitskiy called it "the internal delegation of responsibility." Ibid., p. 30.

Delegation of responsibilities in due course became a core principle of the American human relations policy. This is how Strelbitskiy describes it: "The administrator stands ready to bear responsibility for every detail of his business without putting the blame on Ivan or Peter. However, within his business, he holds that same Ivan or Peter responsible for the situation at the relevant unit. These Ivans and Peters, likewise, divide their responsibility to the manager among their own subordinates yet they are still fully and severely responsible for their work." Ibid.

However, one cannot delegate responsibility by just bossing people around. Every worker must be aware of his role and duties as a member of the production process. How can this be achieved? Managers should foster initiative in their immediate subordinates, expect them to follow suit and enforce this policy at every level. "Even a night watchman should realize that he does not merely stand on guard but performs an important function in the collective adding value."

Therefore, it is important that responsibilities be clearly distributed among all workers. In no instance should a manager do somebody else's work. "Remember, - Strelbitskiy wrote, - this is a mortal sin for an administrator that, regrettably, is still committed time and again." Ibid.

Every member of a work collective should have a clearly delineated area of functions. If the manager wants to do everything himself, if he always "has no time", his business is ill-organized. "The administrator is the main axis of the business for the main cogwheels to revolve around and make other wheels turn. This axis must always be in place and should not try to replace other parts of the mechanism." He gives an example of a gifted manager whom he once visited in his office. "I saw him by the misty window doing nothing else but sketching a rooster! Returning my smile, he said: "If I do the job for all you guys, you would stop working, and I just wouldn't be able to cope." Ibid., p. 31.

Some of the early attempts to formulate the objective laws of management by Russian scholars may seem rather naïve. What is more important, however, is that these scholars were certain such laws existed and needed to be discovered. It is also hard to overstate the value of certain observations that we quote here and that have often been ignored even to this day.

Strelbitskiy also stressed that the most critical and difficult challenge for a manager is to match specific jobs to the right people. Unfortunately, no concrete instructions can exist in this case. Strelbitskiy had many reservations about psychotechnics and believed it could not provide any reliable selection methods, especially for intellectual jobs, where "professional self-determination" has already become a more sound way of choosing appropriate candidates.

Personal inclinations, he thought, are obviously the main factor. Generally speaking, the manager's closest associates should ideally possess the same qualities as himself, i.e., willpower, resolution, steadiness, ingenuity, abstract thinking abilities and so on.

A manager should never bring his old team to the new job. "This policy impairs collective morale and in fact betrays a helpless and hopeless administrator." Ibid., p. 25.

Strelbitskiy makes a good point. Indeed, such an attitude essentially testifies to ineptness in selecting and governing people, as well as the lack of self-confidence. "One must be very narrow-minded, - Strelbitskiy wrote, - to limit trust in people to Ivanov or Petrov whom you met at your previous job. I would deny any administrator a request to bring his "trusted people" to the new job. Moreover, a person making such a request probably has little administrative value. A good administrator is legitimately proud of educating people belonging to "his own school" for the benefit of the economy, of creating good workers rather than chasing them and luring them to new places." Ibid.

This point still holds, since the practice of "dragging" staff remains woefully common.

A proper environment created by the manager in his collective leads to what Strelbitskiy called management automatism. "A system is now in operation, - he wrote, - which means progress is not affected by a "headache" or a lack of energy suffered by a manager. Moreover, the business is not hurt if a worker (especially a manager) leaves; his close associates are capable of continuing his work." Ibid., p. 31.

Strelbitskiy's ideas on this issue are of major interest. In particular, he claimed that once a management system develops an ideal degree of automatism, the manager can painlessly leave the collective for a rather long time. Numerous recent experiments in the USA have confirmed this idea.

4. G.A.Nefedov

Gerasim Alekseevich Nefedov's name is hardly ever mentioned in current works on the history of scientific management. However, he published several papers that offer interesting and useful recommendations pertaining to methodology, theory and practice.

Nefedov did not agree with the idea that management was just an art that could be mastered only by special people. He thought of it as also a science that explores its own laws.[52] True, since these laws have not been established so far, management largely remains an art. Yet it will transform into a science in the near future, with the progress in identifying its laws.

Nefedov paid special attention to the social aspect of management. He identified *three types of organization.*

The simplest organizations that belong to the **first type** have only a single worker who initiates tasks for himself.

---

[52] Nefedov G.A., Office Work. [Kantselyarskoe delo]. Second edition. Moscow-Leningrad, P.8.

The number of workers in organizations of the **second type** is small enough to be managed by just one supervisor.

Organizations of the **third type** have so many employees that they have to be divided in several groups with distinct responsibilities. A single team leader assigns tasks and manages workers within each group. This is how "second-tier" managers appear. Very large groups have in turn to be split in subdivisions headed by "third-tier" managers and so on.

In Nefedov's time organizations and institutions belonged to the second and especially the third type. They usually had several departments, each handling a specific part of the organization's functions. In other words, a growing scale of production calls for deeper division of labor (including managerial labor) and a certain *organizational structure* of the enterprise.[53]

Nefedov maintained that in order to achieve the maximum productivity the enterprise, in particular, should have a sound structure. When a manager gives tasks to workers, *execution is inevitably separated from the initiative.* Indeed, the very communication of the manager's ideas to workers requires some time and energy, even with the use of the best techniques. This is especially true about third-type organizations where initiatives communicated via "second-tier" managers become even more distant from the execution. It is clear, he wrote, that this double (or triple, and so on) transmission, other factors being equal, will take even more time and energy and have a negative impact on productivity.[54]

Nefedov formulated a fundamental principle of management that he called *the basic principle of a structure: the larger is the distance between the initiative and its execution, the lower is the productivity of the organization.* Accordingly, a structure should be designed to bring the manager as close to the executors as the functions of the enterprise and the number of employees permits. "The only way to achieve this goal is to have as few intermediate managers as possible. This, in turn, requires that each manager regardless of his rank

---

[53] Ibid., p. 23.
[54] Ibid., p. 23-24.

46

should supervise the greatest number of subordinates physically possible."[55] Nefedov suggested that a manager should supervise at least 5 workers or lower-level managers or even many more in the case of monotonous, simple or non-urgent work. In any event, an executive should never supervise fewer than 5 subordinates. It makes absolutely no sense for a manager to control a single worker.

Unfortunately, Nefedov wrote little on the upper limit of the "administrative capacity" that appears an even more important (and still outstanding) problem than that of its lower limit.

Nefedov offered valuable insights into areas such as the selection of managers, management style and ethics, managerial qualities required at any level and so on. These are some of his ideas.

He described a good manager as a believer in *democracy,* who can consolidate all team members and inspire the team with a joint impulse to achieve its objectives as fast and as efficiently as possible. In his own words, the manager must, first and foremost, "evoke new energy, set a common pace, coordinate work with other departments and convince everyone that the business is important." The administrator must also foster initiative, persistence, and creativity in his subordinates. "Productivity rises to a new high only when the administrator works hard to make the whole team act, overcome inertia and launch the powerful collective engine of ingenuity."[56]

A good administrator must be nice to his subordinates, continuously learn from them and take advantage of their energy in a broad sense of the word. Many managers owe their success to their ability "to listen to others and check other opinions."[57]

It is critical to grant a maximum of autonomy to subordinates so they can use initiative and be creative. One

---

[55] Ibid., p. 24.
[56] Ibid., p. 33.
[57] Ibid., p. 34.

should avoid giving petty orders that regulate every detail of the subordinate's work. Otherwise, the worker gets used to receiving instructions at every point, and "his brain loses interest in the work and the person just stops caring about the business." Moreover, micromanagement "upsets people and frustrates the regular course of business."[58]

Clear and formal orders also play a role in better productivity. Some managers issue their orders in a hurry, or poorly articulate them, which may lead to confusion. All this betrays "a major lack of managerial talent."

In order to win confidence from subordinates and evoke their initiative, he believed, every suggestion coming from workers must be carefully considered. Reasons for rejection should be communicated to the author, and accepted suggestions should be rewarded. A good work environment is vital; *each and every* worker should be treated "as an important team member rather than something disposable. Lack of respect makes people think of looking for another job, in which case they would never be as useful to the company as they could."[59]

Also, the manager should never think that he knows all the details of a task better than anybody else. Rather than meddling with the execution of his own instructions, he should learn how to distribute all the work among subordinates and restrict himself to control only. Otherwise, he would never have time to deal with strategic issues. Nefedov agreed that a good manager must drop a delusion that no one can do the job better than himself."[60]

Finally, we should note that Vitke and other members of the social trend in management (who were labeled "Russian Fayolists" in the USSR) in fact went even further than Henri Fayol in the exploration of social relations in management. Some of the concepts they formulated have remained valid until today. This new school of managerial thought had great prospects. We regret to say that by the early 1930s the

---

[58] Ibid., p. 35.
[59] Ibid., p. 34.
[60] Ibid., p. 34.

authoritarian and bureaucratic style in Russia won a victory over the school in question.

Chapter 3. How the New Movement Was Destroyed

Most regrettably, the new movement in Soviet Russia was smashed well before coming to fruition, though years later it was brought to life again by Mayo and other American researchers in a far more favorable atmosphere. It was in the USA that these concepts received robust experimental support (Hawthorne) and generally thrived.

An all-out assault was unleashed on the new movement and its leader N.A. Vitke. Even a serious expert such as Academician O.A. Yermanskiy joined the denunciation campaign (only to become a victim himself in due course). To quote one of his irony-laded statements: "A new scientific Gospel proclaims a "theory" by a certain engineer Fayol who founded a "school" with two "careless" disciples Wilbois and Vanuxem who embarked on publishing papers so purely formalist that the works of an idealist such as Tard, with his laws of imitation, seem like a paragon of scientific depth and soundness in comparison."[61]

Ms. E.F. Rozmirovich, a professional revolutionary and a close associate of Lenin himself, became the most tireless and fundamental adversary of the new movement. After the turbulent events in 1917, she found her niche in management studies and even founded the Management Technology Institute. Her vicious attacks eventually led to the destruction of the movement as well as its leader. This criticism was too relentless even by the strictest Communist standards. Was it constructive at all?

---

[61] Yermanskiy O.A., Scientific Management: Status and Objectives. *[Zadachi nauchnoi organizatsii trudsa i ee polozhenie].* "Vestnik Kommunisticheckoi Akademii", 1923, No. 3. P. 181.

As noted above, Vitke rightly maintained that since "industrialism" (large-scale production) required a more sophisticated management system, it suffered "an organizational crisis" as "the available management system was in sharp conflict with the scale and nature of work to be performed."[62] Vitke believed this crisis could be addressed by an "organizational revolution" that would replace personal discretion, intuition and "universalism" in management with scientific principles pertaining to sociology rather than technology. These views sparked strong protests. Rozmirovich saw them as a sword raised against "the holy of holies", i.e., the Marxist-Leninist principles underlying her own "production-based approach". It was at this point that she started her unfair criticism.

First of all, she challenged the idea that a machine in itself is blind and dead, so its potential can fully materialize only as a result of intelligent human (social and industrial) organization. As Vitke further developed this concept by emphasizing the role of the "social engineer" (a new profession born with industrialism) as opposed to the regular engineer incapable of solving organizational problems, Rozmirovich was getting more and more indignant. She saw no connection whatsoever between large-scale industry and the emergence of a special group of administrators. Carried away with enthusiasm, she claimed that even the capitalist society had no need for any such administrators.[63]

The idea of administration as a special integrating function of management incensed Rozmirovich so much that she branded Vitke with a sarcastic nickname of "a Russian Fayolist." Fayol indeed maintained that such activities were becoming autonomous, though this idea is hardly a vulnerable

---

[62] Vitke N.A., Organization of Management and Industrial Development. *(Organizatsiya upravleniya i industrialnoe razvitie.)* P. 40.
[63] Rozmirovich E.F., On Certain "Scientific" Management Theories in Government and Industry. *[O nekotorykh "nauchnykh" teoriyakh upravleniya gosudarstvennymi uchrezhdeniyami I predpriyatiyami.]* Sotsialisticheskoe khozyaistvo. 1925, No. 1. P. 219, 226 etc.

point in Vitke's theory. Quite the opposite: The fact that he expanded on Fayol's discussion on administration shows that Vitke identified some positive elements in the French doctrine that could not be ignored.

If even the idea of an autonomous administration function exasperated Rozmirovich, the assumption that such a function has an increasing significance in the new economy made her almost hysterical. It is hard to agree with her arguments, however. Vitke distinguished between the administrator and the technical executor, i.e., between the management of things and that of people. He stressed that "a lack of insight into this difference may lead to major blunders."[64] Rozmirovich, on the other hand, never recognized this difference in her "production-based approach." Yet the idea of similarity between production and management makes sense only if it is not carried to extremes when the social content of manufacturing is dismissed altogether and overwhelmed by the "technical" approach. Rozmirovich, in fact, advocated a primitive concept of management and claimed that management of people in a developed economy would vanish by "dissolving" in the management of things. *We have to admit that Rozmirovich's criticism was far from convincing; moreover, it was outright destructive.* Vitke was correct when he made the above warning against the perils of underestimating the social aspects of personnel management. Industrial management is primarily the management of people, teams and human relations that take shape in the course of collective labor. In a developed society with a sophisticated economy the significance of management, particularly personnel management, is indeed growing exactly like Vitke and his like-minded colleagues suggested.

Vitke was also violently criticized for promoting psychological methods of affecting "human labor collectives." Today, when such methods have proven to be just as effective as economic, legal and other counterparts, those accusations seem particularly unfair. Moreover, *Vitke should be given credit for raising the very issue of social and psychological laws of manufacturing.* He reasoned that "the behavior of any

---

[64] Vitke N.A., Issues in Management. P. 22.

collective... is based on some social and psychological laws. Once these laws are discovered and mastered, this work collective could be designed to function at a maximum efficiency as a true social machine."[65]

Finally, the idea of a special science of managing people (that is now self-evident) was also smashed by Vitke's opponents.[66] According to Rozmirovich, this concept "means a clean break with Marxism, a pretense to build a distinct applied discipline based on naked psychology and psychological experiments, which throws us back into the swamp of old-fashioned idealistic babble... Marxism knows nothing about any psychological science of managing people... moreover, even the idea of such a science is a pointless and dangerous Utopian proposition... a piece of reactionary nonsense that Marxists have been and will be resolutely against."

According to Rozmirovich, something that "Marxism knows nothing about" obviously cannot exist at all. Rozmirovich defends Marxism in strong words. Vitke's theory, she writes "seems like a pathetic repetition of socialist-revolutionary fantasies," since it "consistently advocates ... anti-Marxist and unscientific views..."[67]

The worst was that Rozmirovich's accusations tended to be ideological and *political.* Her immense political clout and proximity to high government circles (Lenin, Kuybyshev and certainly Krylenko, her husband) made her criticism truly dangerous. Indeed, by the late 1920's Vitke's name already disappeared from the literature for many decades. His plight is still unknown, though most likely he was killed during the purges like many of his like-minded colleagues. The social theme in management theory was banned, and Russian

---

[65] Vitke N.A., Organization of Management and Industrial Development. P.178.

[66] See, e.g., Rozmirovich E.F., The Results of RKI work on NOT [K itogam raboty RKI po NOT]. "Voprosy sovetskogo khozyaistva I upravleniya", 1924, No. 4-5. P. 115-116.

[67] The Beginning of NOT. Forgotten Discussions and Ideas that Never Came to Life. Ed. by E.B. Koritskiy.

scientific management now lags by more than half a century behind its Western counterpart - that made the greatest achievements precisely in the area castigated by Rozmirovich and Bolsheviks at large.

We quoted the basic points of Vitke's critics in order to show, first, that his theory has to be reassessed and second, to better demonstrate its merits.

All of the above certainly does not mean that Vitke's principles are invincible. Some of them are indeed doubtful or even invalid; they certainly need an impartial scientific discussion.

In particular, Vitke and his followers at times *disproportionately inflated the significance of the socio-psychological approach to management.* Important as it is, a good psychological climate at the workplace cannot be the overarching objective of a manager. Vitke, on the other hand, maintained that "this approach to social work cooperation gives all the power to scientific management. It reveals the essence of the task, rationalizes the blind empirical process and gives the right direction to the **entire** work..."[68] As we see, Vitke and his followers are indeed inclined to discount the economic and other aspects of management.

This was a reason for certain flaws in Vitke's attempts to clearly identify the science of management. While realizing its interdisciplinary character, he *places this science at the border between disciplines such as "industrial and collective psychology", "structural sociology" or physiology while largely ignoring economics, jurisprudence, political science and other fields of knowledge.*[69]

On the whole, however, let us reiterate that Vitke's concepts, despite their occasional inconsistence and immaturity, are highly valuable because they *focus on social aspects, emphasize the human factor in management, raise*

---

[68] Vitke N.A., Scientific Organization of Management Technology. P. 15.
[69] Vitke N.A., Organization of Management and Industrial Development. P. 132-133.

major new issues and address them in an innovative way. These concepts have stood the test of time. It is our duty today to talk about their forgotten authors to restore historical justice and take advantage of them in order to catch up in this historically neglected area of science.

Part II. Selected works by N.A. Vitke and their critical review

1. N.A. Vitke, "Organization of Management and Industrial Development"

Chapter I. The Origins of NOT

1. The right approach to NOT

The Russian revolution has apparently entered a new stage of development, that of *constructing* a new economy, governance system and culture. These new times mean new challenges. *Issues of labor management* are high on this agenda. Hence a keen interest in the so called NOT (scientific organization of labor and management). Over the past year, NOT has emerged from relative obscurity as a subject of numerous publications, presentations, and discussions. Efforts on systematic introduction of NOT in the USSR have already involved a variety of organizations such as research institutes, labor improvement departments (experimental stations and management bureaus), non-governmental organizations (the Time League, the Red Directors Club, the Engineers' Association, the nascent union of administrators), a special Commissariat (Workers' and Peasants' Inspectorate) and one of the highest governing bodies of the Party, namely the Central Control Commission (**1**).

Despite all this sudden and broad popularity, a multitude of participating organizations and a direct interest from high Party and government quarters, however, the issue of NOT still seems to be lacking clarity. No one appears to be sure about its social nature, applicability limits, implementation techniques and relevance to the construction of the Soviet system.

The reason, we believe, is that the current approach to NOT is dominated by two equally extreme and equally flawed trends. Some thinkers regard NOT as mostly or exclusively a doctrine, a teaching or a system. This is an *ideological approach* whose supporters concentrate on various disagreements among schools and trends, clash with fellow theoreticians and develop their own "ideologies". At the same time, they pay scant attention to the practical side of NOT, generalization becomes a self-contained goal for such scholars, live links with the actual participants in the movement are broken, historical perspective is lost – in short, the true fundamentals of the movement are largely ignored for the sake of identifying theoretical differences between various NOT schools and developing an integral NOT theory, even if it would be premature at this time.

This extreme trend, so obviously biased and inadequate, has been predominant so far in the Russian literature on NOT.

The second trend, that is equally biased and inadequate, has recently emerged as a reaction to the first one and appears to be gaining momentum. This approach is based on *narrow pragmatism*. We believe it is too naïve to be long-lived in its present form. Its supporters tend to preach improvement of elementary work habits rather than mastering true work culture. In terms of practice, this trend aims to cover an almost infinite and ill-defined area, as well as to reduce the entire NOT movement to practical applications only. Any improvement in labor management is labeled a NOT achievement, while any research into NOT is utterly dismissed.

While the first (ideological) trend suffers from being too abstract and too theoretical, while it narrows the NOT basis down to a laboratory or an academic study, the second trend goes too far in the opposite direction by replacing learned theories and science-based applications with the need for elementary literacy, by reducing vital management issues to crude technical prescriptions. In fact, this trend wants to take advantage of NOT applications without any research efforts and expands the area of NOT to unreasonable limits when it becomes impossible to figure out the job description of a NOT expert and decide whether a particular issue belongs to NOT.

Both trends are obviously limited and inadequate. Clearly, an improvement in administration practices or work techniques does not necessarily result from scientific management. It is equally clear that any meaningful introduction of NOT is impossible without research and theoretical work, much like therapy or surgery are unthinkable without clinics, laboratories and sophisticated scientific investigations. Clearly, "NOT literacy" is a far cry from NOT; likewise, if any knowledgeable manager can be considered a NOT expert, then brushing your teeth is all the hygiene one needs, avoiding unboiled water makes one a doctor and fixing a door knob turns one into a cabinet maker.

Something else is very obvious as well. NOT is not limited to a laboratory or the academy. While being a theory (or, rather, a cluster of theories), NOT is also a public movement that has very real practical supporters and stems from very real practical conditions.

So, prior to any broad practical implementation of NOT in the USSR, prior to any inevitable integration of the two biased approaches that currently prevail, one ought to ask a number of questions. What is NOT as a public movement? Why did it emerge? What is the direction of its progress? What does it have in common with the Russian revolution and the issues of building socialism? What position does it occupy among other kinds of struggle for a superior work culture? What is the relation between NOT theory and practice?

We shall strive to answer these questions below.

2. Industry as the cradle of NOT

NOT comes from the same cradle as all the other broad cultural movements of today such as modern technology, modern science and modern scientific socialism, that is, from *industry*.

It was the metal industry that gave birth to Taylorism **(2)** and Fordism **(3).** Moreover, both theories emerged during the period of intense and rapid concentration and cartelization of this industry late in the XIX century. The "broad NOT" of the French school of experimental administration led by the engineer Fayol **(4)** who challenged government

57

administration, the army, trade, educational, political and other social management systems to "industrialize" is also rooted in industry.

Industry is the cradle of modern NOT. This does not mean just factories, however. It means *the industrial society*. Modern industry has revolutionized everything: It has changed means of transportation, urban and rural lifestyles, and the system of government, the attitudes, and philosophy of all members of society.

Likewise, NOT, the offspring of industry, is now bound to revolutionize the work of every single labor collective in the industrial society. Since the beginning of this century it has been spreading from industry to retail and wholesale trade. The 1914 World War led to the spontaneous penetration of NOT to every area of collective labor as well as to the launch of a conscious slogan "to industrialize". Even conservative countries such as France or Belgium are revamping their government agencies on advice from NOT experts.

What are the causes of this broad movement in the industrial society? Who are its practical supporters? What are its practical implications?

3. Concentration of industry

The emergence of NOT is closely associated with one of the most fundamental and powerful natural processes in the capitalist society, that is, the concentration of production (and, more generally, collective labor).

Recent decades have seen an ever-accelerating large-scale concentration of human masses and means of production to form major enterprises. Smaller factories are dying out fast to give way to giant industrial companies (Krupp, Siemens, Ford and the like) with tens of thousands of workers; mammoth retail companies such as Kaiser's Kaffee Geschäft with 1,500 branches, Wertheim in Berlin with 5,000 employees or the Hamburg America Steamship with over 15,000 employees; large financial institutions, e.g., Disconto Bank (533,000 incoming and 626,000 outgoing transactions a year),

Credit Lyonnaise that opens 633,500 accounts a year, or Deutsche Bank that employs about 26,000 people.

The number of employees at Deutsche Bank was:

1910 - 5,800

1920 - 17,800

1921 - 21,137

1922 - 26,268

The following figures on England give an idea of concentration in the banking sector.

Number of branches in 1923:

1. London and Westminster Bank............................914

2. National Provincial and Union Bank..................1 090

3. London Joint City and Midland Bank.................1 740

4. Lloyds Bank...1 600

5. Barclays Bank...1 700

_____

7 044

The United States Government Life Insurance (USGLI) in 1917 received 40 million letters and employed 17,000 people. Its sorting boxes arranged in a straight line would have a length of 5 miles. The French Ministry of Foreign Affairs receives over 100,000 letters a day and so does the Ministry of Home Affairs in London.

In the United States of America, 1% of factories by 1909 accounted for 30.5% of workers and 44% of industrial output. In Germany by 1907 less than 1% of enterprises employed about 40% of the total workforce and consumed 75% of steam power and about 80% of electric power.

The process of concentration is not limited to the emergence of large production facilities, however. It also leads to *separation of management from ownership, to depersonalization of capital and strong centralization of enterprise management.*

As factory management separates from ownership, it becomes a distinct *profession* of special hired employees. This separation and the emergence of professional managers is caused not only by the predominance of large and sophisticated production facilities but also by a number of other current economic trends. The prevalence of public companies, trusts and syndicates, on the one hand, the increasing power of banking capital, on the other hand, as well as the growing economic activity of cooperative, municipal and state-owned enterprises lead to *enormous concentration of economic management* and also requires a special profession of organizers and administrators with their own office clerks and assistants at various levels.

For instance, in 1895 Germany had 1028 corporations with 66,000 employees compared to 17,180 with 2.5 million employees by 1907. There were also about 9.5 thousand municipal, state-owned and other public enterprises with about 0.5 million workers. In total, corporation-type companies in Germany in 2007 employed about 3 million people or about 25% of all industrial workers.

Development of joint-stock companies in Germany

Year	Number	Capital, million DM
1886-	2,143	4,876
1907-08	4,578	12,788
1911-12	4,712	14,800
1922	9,812	110,000

The share of sole-proprietor wool spinneries in England decreased from 77% in 1884 to just 16% in 1914, while the share of partnerships and public companies in the industry increased from 23% to 84%. Corporate ownership in the weaving industry increased from 9% in 1884 to 52% in 1914.

Development of joint-stock companies in England.

	Number	Capital, £ mln
1884	8 694	500
1912	56 362	2 420
1918	66 882	2 900
1922	84 101	4 180

In the USA in 1919, 31.5% of companies that accounted for over 86% of the workforce and 88% of annual output belonged to various corporations, primarily joint-stock companies, rather than sole proprietors.

Development of public corporations in the USA

(% of the total).

	Companies.	Employees	Annual output
1904	23.6	70.6	73.7
1909	25.9	75.6	79.0
1914	26.3	80.3	83.2
1919	31.5	86.6	87.8

These data illustrate the process of *"depersonalization of capital"*. The enormous extent of *concentration* of capital and management is evidenced, for example, by the fact that the Rhenish-Westphalian Syndicate in 1907 produced 95.4% of all coal in Germany.

The sugar syndicate accounted for 70% of domestic sales and 80% of exports of this commodity. The General Electricity Company, a union of Siemens, Rhine, Elba and Schuckert established after the war by Stinnes, has 872 individual enterprises, 968 factories and a capital of 14.5 billion golden deutschemarks.

The transnational harvester company in the USA accounted for the production of 76.6% of mowers and 87% of sheaf binders by 1911. The steel trust produced 83% of cast pipes, 78% of wire and 80% of black sheet iron. The oil trust had a system of pipelines 40,000 miles long and produced 86% of lamp oil in the USA.

By the end of 1909 the nine largest Berlin banks with a number of smaller affiliates owned 83% of all the banking capital in Germany and essentially controlled the entire national economy. For instance, we have found that three large banks had their representatives at 750 major enterprises.

This concentration process is well-known. However, it is usually analyzed in political or socio-economic terms.

At the same time, it produces a major impact on the *organization of society*, if only because it generates a unique *professional* group of hired managers.

4. Concentration of economic activities and division of labor

The concentration of economic activities occurs simultaneously with the process of sophisticated and detailed division of labor and deep specialization.

Data on the classification of professions from German censuses can give an idea of this process.

Number of professions according to national censuses.

	1882	1895	Increase, %
A. Agriculture, horticulture, animal husbandry, forestry and fisheries	352	465	32
B. Mining, metallurgy, manufacturing and construction	2,661	5,106	103,1
C. Trade and transportation	1,215	2,266	86.5
D. Home services and general labor	75	82	9.3
E. Military, Royal Court, public service, clergy, self-employed	1,876	2,079	10.8
Total	6,179	10,298	66.6

As evidenced by this table, the increase in the number of professions was the most dramatic in trade and transportation (+86.5%) and industry (+103.1%), e.g., from 300 to 708 in metal working and from 182 to 331 in the chemical industry.

German statisticians identified 6179, 10298 and 14000 professions in 1882, 1895 and 1907 respectively. The 1901 British census identified 15,000 professions. According to Petrenz, there were 25 basic professions with 68 subtypes in Leipzig between 1830 and 1860; by 1890 these numbers increased to 42 and 172 respectively.

The process of division of labor, however, cannot be reduced to deeper differentiation and specialization. It also involves *integration* of individual workers with large entities by means of administration centers.

It is fairly obvious that managing a dozen workers is a far cry from managing hundreds of thousands, especially if a small team consists of *similar* workers, and a hundred thousand represents *a number of different qualifications.*

While leaving aside the issue of various management methods for the time being, we still need to note that as an organization increases the scale of operations, as it gets more sophisticated and intrinsically heterogeneous in terms of various professions, it has a growing need in a complex *administration structure* that would *consolidate* the entire organization, harmonize its heterogeneous parts and make them move towards a common goal in strict cooperation, systematically, quickly and with a minimum of friction between parts.

The concentration of labor brings about the problem of rational *differentiation* (division) of labor as well as that of rational *integration* (unification) of labor. Accordingly, each organization has to deal with two groups of issues: the physical and the social division of labor.

5. The management function becomes a profession

The social division of labor with the aim of integrating all work processes is a function of the management system. As this function becomes more independent and professional in larger and more complex organizations, it requires independent *professional organizers and administrators.*

This is why the decrease in the number of sole proprietors is accompanied by an even greater increase in the number of managers and their assistants.

Here are some statistics for Germany (per 100 people)

	1882	1895	1907
a) *Industry and mining*:			
Principals (owners and directors)	34.5	25.0	17.5
Workers	64.0	71.9	76.3
Management	1.5	3.1	6.2
b) *Trade and transportation*:			

Principals (owners and directors)	44.7	36.0	23.1
Workers	46.3	52.7	56.3
Management	9.0	11.3	14.6

Administration requires a sophisticated support system. This is why at advanced enterprises *the proportion of management-related staff* has been growing compared to that of workers.

Levenstern reported that Putilov Works used to have 1 manager per 64.5 workers. In late 1917, the Moscow industrial zone had one manager per 22.5 workers in the textile industry and 10.5 workers in the metallurgical industry. The Russian metal-working industry, as evidenced by Grinevetskiy, had one manager per 10-15 or more workers. Large enterprises in post-war Germany and the United States employ one manager per 7 and 6 workers respectively.

Ludwig Loewe's arms factories before the war had 1 manager per 4.5 workers. Yermanskiy **(5)**, who visited a number of large and well-equipped German factories, reports that this proportion currently equals 1:5. As is well-known, Taylor believes that ideally it should reach 1:3.

Of great interest is the following table:

Relative increase in the number of entrepreneurs, workers and office workers in the US industry:

	1899	**1904**	**1909**
Entrepreneurs	100	106	128
Workers	100	116	140
Office staff	100	142	217

The increase in wages and salaries testifies to the same trend.

Increase in wage bill:

Workers	100%	130%	176%
Office staff	100%	150 %	246%

Data from the German industry are even more impressive.

Relative increase in the number of workers, office staff and engineers in the German economy:

	1882	1895	1907
Workers	100	149	218
Office staff	100	219	498
Engineers	100	250	575

The specific data for industry are as follows:

Relative increase in the number of workers, office staff and engineers in the German industry:

	1895	1907
Workers	100	143
Office staff	100	290
Technicians	100	230
Senior engineers (excluding senior management, since no figures are available for	100	255

1895)

In total, the German industry in 1907 employed 8.5 million workers, 58.3 thousand senior managers, 125.4 thousand engineers, 241 thousand technicians and 318.5 thousand office staff.

6. Management in the army

Industrialization and concentration lead to similar results in the economy as well as elsewhere. For instance, the above-mentioned trends in industrial organization such as an increase in specialization and the relative number of managers are obvious in today's army.

The modern army is a giant destruction factory. As any factory, it is based on sophisticated machinery. The army is industrializing. The share of its technology-based components such as artillery, sapper units and the air force is ever-increasing, and specialization follows suit. At the same time, the management system grows in scope and significance. This dual process of technological differentiation and integration-oriented management covers infantry as well as technology-based units. For instance, the primary combat unit in the French army consists of 13 people. These include three officers (unit commander, riflemen commander and machine gun unit commander). Out of the remaining 10 people five perform various functions (machine gunner, observer, grenade thrower, ammunition carrier and messenger). Only the remaining five have one and the same function of riflemen.

The German army used to have one officer per 44 soldiers in 1882 and 39 soldiers in 1911; now it has one officer per 27 soldiers. There were 6 soldiers per petty officer in 1911, now this number is 4.5. Overall, a German regiment today has 71 officers, 435 petty officers, and 1200 privates. A military author observes that "a company allocates 25 people to command duties and has 15 to 20 messengers, i.e., about 18%

of its combat personnel. In a 1647-strong regiment that consists of 9 companies, 451 people (about 28%) are responsible for command and communications. In other words, one out of four servicemen in a regiment deals exclusively with management. If we continue by adding management and communications personnel at all staffs including General Staff and consider that combat units routinely have vacancies, the number of managers could well be almost equal to that of subordinates. Mankind, however, has to make these sacrifices because otherwise thousands and millions of people would be just a crowd that could hardly be moved and deployed to say nothing of waging a war.

7. NOT needs to establish a new professional group of organizers and administrators

The general meaning of the above is quite clear. One of the fundamental features of industrial development, i.e., the dual process that involves concentration of production and differentiation (division, specialization) of labor, has brought about, apart from a number of new manufacturing professions, *a distinct social profession* of an organizer and administrator. During the XIX century enterprise owners were gradually delegating day-to-day management of various technological processes to special skilled employees. Likewise, since the end of the XIX century we have been witnessing the transfer of strategic control over the entire production process at an enterprise to professional managers. Concentrated production makes such executives responsible for addressing a complex challenge of organizing and leading the collective labor of an economic agent.

NOT abroad has been essentially created by this new group of professional organizers and administrators at large enterprises. This theoretical and practical movement focuses on developing a rational system of management in the industry and other sectors that use collective labor. To this end, the movement is trying to build up a special science (or, rather, several special sciences) of management, much like other disciplines emerged to support specific technological and economic activities. Note that the term NOT (scientific organization of labor) is – both formally and in terms of meaning – a wrong translation of the corresponding foreign term *scientific office management and administration* [term used by the author in English – Translator's note].

One should not think that NOT appeared suddenly and instantly in the heads of Taylor, Emerson **(6),** Fayol or some other theoreticians. This movement has evolved as a spontaneous lengthy process that features two distinct trends closely connected in practice, i.e., the *systematic empirical improvement* and the *scientific improvement* of the administration function.

The former trend appeared and developed somewhat earlier than the latter. It has emerged directly and spontaneously, by means of unnoticeable innovations born by everyday practices. The brightest and most experienced practical organizers in specific areas of the economy are hired by various institutions as ad hoc or full-time consultants. Due to the above-mentioned concentration of production as well as fierce competition, a distinct profession of management consultants has gradually appeared in industrial European countries in response to high demand. Large firms are established to deal with this business. Take, for instance, Orga Actien Gesellschaft in Germany, the Shaw Co. in the USA, and the US affiliates of well-known companies such as Knoeppel or Emerson. These companies have been active as corporate consultants, restructuring experts, trainers and publishers. (For instance, the print run of *System – The Business Magazine* published by Shaw Co. has increased from 2,000 to 40,000 over 25 years of existence.) A prominent element of this movement is the Office for the Audit of Cooperative Societies that does not restrict itself to financial and general control but sets a clear goal of providing direct management consultations and assistance to cooperatives. The same function is performed in the USA by professional auditors in trust companies and numerous industrial "systematizers" who use comparative analysis of spreadsheets in similar industries to streamline corporate management.

This movement for *systematic empirical improvement* of management is based on raw experience, does not rise to general conclusions or create any theoretical systems. It amounts to a mechanical sum of certain theoretical rules and expertise (say, in accounting of banking) needed by a practicing organizer and held together by his empirical intuition and industry-specific management experience rather than by a logical scientific theory.

This initiative has done a lot of preparatory work for its higher and better organized counterpart, a movement for the scientific improvement of management that emerged and developed (approximately until the 1914 war) almost entirely within industry. It reflects the philosophy, the interests and concerns of an industrial manager. It has been dominated by engineers' unions who naturally sought to take advantage of scientific methods, develop the general principles of management and link this field of applied science to the entire current body of scientific knowledge.

Taylor can be called the founder of scientific management but with certain reservations. In fact, he was just the most tenacious, consistent, talented and broad-minded representative of American engineers' quest for a better management in the late XIX century. In fact, the scientific management movement started to formulate its objectives 10 years before Taylor's first public presentation and 18 years before he published the first finished draft of his system.

The very first presentation at the American Society of Mechanical Engineers that started the movement had already defined its goals and its socio-economic significance. We refer to Henri Towne's speech in 1886 where he advocated the need for mechanical engineers to deal with management issues.

In his presentation Towne made the following points. The success of an enterprise and, therefore, its engineering personnel, is measured by the amount of dividends paid. Profitability, however, depends on much more than state-of-the art machinery, that is, on many issues related to the management system. Therefore, an engineer cannot limit himself to technological problems. He should expand the range of his habitual interests and concentrate on complicated and critical aspects of management.

The ASME agreed with the presentation, amended its Articles of Association and commenced research into management.

It was at this point that the movement for scientific management at enterprises and institutions started its steady (though occasionally intermittent) progress.

In 1920, scientific management societies in the USA had 4041 member (see table below):

ASME management section	1 740
Society of Industrial Engineering	1 032
The Taylor Society	769
National Association of Business Administration	500
Total	4041

About half of these 4,000 people joined the above societies over the past two years. It is interesting to note that 120 out of 500 members of the National Association of Business Administration represent manufacturing or trade corporations.

Both in the USA and in continental Europe the scientific management movement has its practical agents. These administrators in manufacturing and other industries are called Verwaltungsingenieurs in German and efficiency engineers in English; they have established the National Union of German Administration Organizers. It is also accompanied with a broader movement that challenges current technology-focused engineering curricula and insists on a slogan *Ingenieur als Volkswirt* (engineer as an economist) that emphasizes the importance of general economic and sociological training for administrators/organizers.

Chapter II. Organizational Crisis in Large-scale Production

1. *The cultural relevance of NOT*

We have established that (1) the concentration of management in manufacturing (and other labor) collectives in the industrial society has given rise to a distinct profession of organizers and administrators with an appropriate support system and (2) it was this new professional group that started a scientific and practical movement for the organization of management and labor in foreign countries, with factory administrators as its practical agents.

This movement proclaims no direct broad goals in political or cultural terms. Its principal objective is different and rather narrow. It endeavors to help the professional administrator in his day-to-day practical work by making it as *scientific* as that of today's medical doctors, agronomists, process engineers (in a broad sense) and so on.

While NOT goals may appear limited and highly specific, this movement is in fact a major and even revolutionary cultural factor.

The activities of professional administrators mean a break with individualism, *autocracy* and the closely related *traditionalism* in everyday work, and the elimination of something that Americans today regard as the main barrier to sound organization, i.e., *individual views and habits* that should give way to *planning and collectivism*.

In the environment created by the above-mentioned concentration of management, professional administrators as a group struggle with individualism in the economy for two reasons. The first reason is that concentrated economic activities demand consistent and rigorous accounting as well as planning. The second reason is the famous *human factor* in the large-scale industry.

2. Industrialism requires organization as well as machinery

Industrialism is essentially based on machinery. A large-scale enterprise must use state-of-the-art machines. However, perfect machines alone do not necessarily make a perfect enterprise. Organizational work is just as vital to industrialism as machine design. A machine in itself is blind and dead. Its potential can fully materialize only as a result of intelligent human (social and industrial) organization. Therefore, industrialism raises several unique new *organizational* issues.

Machines must be used to full capacity. This is the first and foremost rule of large-scale production. Downtime of any duration and for whatever reasons causes a direct loss to the enterprise and makes it less competitive.

This explains both interconnected trends typical of modern large-scale manufacturing, i.e., towards mass production of similar goods and towards tight integration and continuity of processes.

The economic advantages of mass production are obvious.

American entrepreneurs made the following estimates of production costs for a spare part:

Number of parts made	Cost, cents
1	25
2	15
5	10
100	5
500	2

The cost of making a pair of shoes at a Moscow factory is as follows:

Number of pairs made	Cost, rubles
500	33
2,000	12.80
3,000	9.80
4,000	8.80
10,000	6.80

The ultimate application of the mass production principle is when the whole factory moves to manufacturing a single product. This ensures (1) the optimum (most sound) and continuous use of available machinery and (2) utmost customization of machinery and work techniques to meet specific production needs.

A sophisticated manufacturing process such as shipbuilding provides a graphic example.

As estimated by a competent author, the cost of building a steamship is as follows:

Number of ships ordered	cost, DM	Savings, DM	%
1	1,624,000	-	-
2	1,580,000	44,000	2.7
3	1,560,000	64,000	4.0
4	1,544,000	80,000	4.9

The author also indicates that standardization of certain spare parts for steamships can provide 6% in additional savings. Accordingly, mass production of one steamship model results in savings of at least 11%.

Apart from cost advantages, mass production also means faster delivery.

Here is an impressive story that once made headlines and attracted public attention to the issues of standardization for the first time. The British army in the Sudan urgently needed a railway bridge to be constructed. European companies offered to do the job in at least a year and a half. A company from Philadelphia, however, offered to build the bridge in a few weeks' time. This commitment was met on schedule because the company had a stock of standard parts that were delivered to the site and quickly assembled.

Ford is capable of delivering 6,500 inexpensive cars a day precisely because he manufactures just one model and his mammoth company of 70,000 employees is fully specialized and adapted to accomplish this single task.

The trend towards mass production of similar goods has been gaining momentum fast. A large British car maker used to manufacture 26 car models. Now they advertise their product as "the only model we make".

The Taylor Society reports the following figures regarding the scope of standardization in New York over the past few years:

Product	Number of models before and after standardization	
	before	after
1.Drilling machines	784	29
2.Plows	589	38
3.Pocket knives	6000	129
4.Toothed gear for agricultural machinery	1736	16

3.   *Marx on the cooperative nature of machine labor*

"In simple cooperation, and even in that founded on the division of labor, the suppression of the isolated, by the collective, workman still appears to be more or less accidental. Machinery, with a few exceptions to be mentioned later, operates only by means of associated labor, or labor in common. Hence the cooperative character of the labor process is, in the latter case, a technical necessity dictated by the instrument of labor itself," Marx wrote.

The cooperative nature of machine labor is more than evident now. The entire movement of professional organizers and administrators essentially aims at promoting labor cooperation because machinery "operates only by means of associated labor".

In this area the modern world faces a major challenge that disarms the engineer and has to be tackled by new professionals, the *organizers.* This challenge faced by any large-scale manufacturing company is *to ensure the coherence and continuity of an enormous number of detail workers* whose aggregate forms what Marx called "a social worker" at a given facility and what we shall call, for our technical purposes, *"the production chain of detail workers".*

In his description of manufacture Marx notes the following in this regard: "Since the fractional product of each detail laborer is, at the same time, only a particular stage in the development of one and the same finished article, each laborer, or each group of laborers, prepares the raw material for another laborer or group. The result of the labor of the one is the starting-point for the labor of the other. The one workman therefore gives occupation directly to the other. The labor-time necessary in each partial process, for attaining the desired effect, is learnt by experience; and the mechanism of Manufacture, as a whole, is based on the assumption that a given result will be obtained in a given time. It is only on this assumption that the various supplementary labor-processes can proceed uninterruptedly, simultaneously, and side by side. It is clear that this direct dependence of the operations, and therefore of the laborers, on each other, compels each one of them to spend on his work no more than the necessary time, and thus a continuity, uniformity, regularity, order, and even intensity of labor, of quite a different kind, is begotten than is to be found in an independent handicraft or even in simple cooperation. The rule, that the labor-time expended on a commodity should not exceed that which is socially necessary for its production, appears, in the production of commodities generally, to be established by the mere effect of competition; since, to express ourselves superficially, each single producer is obliged to sell his commodity at its market-price. In Manufacture, on the contrary, the turning out of a given quantum of product in a given time is a technical law of the process of production itself."

"Different operations take, however, unequal periods, and yield therefore, in equal times unequal quantities of fractional products. If, therefore, the same laborer has, day after day, to perform the same operation, there must be a different number of laborers for each operation; for instance, in type manufacture, there are four founders and two breakers to one rubber: The founder casts 2,000 types an hour, the breaker breaks up 4,000, and the rubber polishes 8,000. Here we have again the principle of cooperation in its simplest form, the simultaneous employment of many doing the same thing; only now, this principle is the expression of an organic relation. The division of labor, as carried out in Manufacture, not only simplifies and multiplies the qualitatively different parts of the social collective laborer, but also creates a fixed mathematical relation or ratio which regulates the quantitative extent of those parts i.e., the relative number of laborers, or the relative size of the group of laborers, for each detail operation."

Marx provides specific examples of "production chains of detail laborers" in the manufacture of watches (11 persons) and needles (72 and 92 persons).

Marx was talking about manufacture. His observations, however, fully apply to large-scale industrial production, where the same laws just become more significant and complicated. "The turning out of a given quantum of product in a given time is a technical law of the process of production itself", at a modern plant it is certainly true even to a greater and more rigorous extent than at a manufacture. At the same time, this law can hardly be implemented at a modern production facility merely on the basis of "simple experience" without meticulous research and the use of scientific methods.

"In Manufacture, the organization of the social labor-process is purely subjective; it is a combination of detail laborers; in its machinery system, modern industry has a productive organism that is purely objective, in which the laborer becomes a mere appendage to an already existing material condition of production. In simple cooperation, and even in that founded on division of labor, the suppression of the isolated, by the collective, workman still appears to be more or less accidental. *Machinery, with a few exceptions to be mentioned later, operates only by means of associated labor, or labor in common. Hence the cooperative character of the labor-process is, in the latter case, a technical necessity dictated by the instrument of labor itself.*"

4. Sound cooperation among detail workers as the central problem of modern industrial manufacturing

As we have mentioned above, one of the key economic principles of manufacturing is that machinery must be used to its full capacity. Any downtime of any duration for whatever reasons causes a direct loss to the enterprise and makes it less competitive.

We have also noted a new unqualified requirement to the production that follows from this law, i.e., *an enterprise must be based on tight integration and continuity of all partial production processes.*

In other words, production cooperation among partial workers at an enterprise must be designed as *a continuous integrated chain of work* with a *continuous flow of products along this chain.* We could also say that an enterprise must be designed and run as an integral mechanism whose smallest

78

cogwheel starts action at a precisely calculated moment and makes a revolution as fast as technology permits.

Organization of an integrated production process by thousands of detail workers with dissimilar skills on the basis of a continuous manufacturing flow and maximum coordination among all members of the production chain is a task brought to the top of the agenda by the process of industrial development.

This task is far more urgent and difficult than during the manufacture period. Indeed:

1) The above mentioned fundamental economic law of manufacturing leads to mass production of uniform goods where a smallest advantage or mistake is multiplied by a factor of thousands with dramatic ramifications.

2) The partial specialization described in Chapter 1 creates extremely long and thin production chains.

The following data testify to the importance of these factors.

Over a period of 13 years in Germany the number of specialized professions increased from 300 to 708 in metal-working, from 335 to 653 in machine-building and from 182 to 331 in the chemical industry.

In the American meat-packing industry an animal carcass consecutively passes through the hands of 157 workers who manage to "process" 1,000 head of cattle a day. Motor assembly at the Ford Company is now performed by 84 people rather than one worker but takes 5 hours 56 minutes instead of 10 hours as before. A magneto is assembled by 29 workers in 5 minutes. On the whole, the manufacturing flow at Ford factories passes through the hands of 70,000 detail workers to produce 6,500 cars a day. A Ford car consists of 5,600 parts manufactured at 500 company factories. The manufacturing flow moves along the chain of more than 15,000 detail workers.

3) When the production chain is designed, one has to take into account not only the worker, as at a manufacture, but to construct the entire "objective" (as Marx put it) "production

organism", i.e., select the necessary machines and place them in strict order to ensure a continuous manufacturing process.

Sometimes this results in a complete departure from the traditional structure of a factory. Say, Ford's production units are not organized by the type of machinery and tools as turning shops, forgeries, assembly shops and the like. Rather, every shop manufactures a product from beginning to end. A future car part comes to a shop as raw material or a crude cast, passes through a number of processing stages (including hot treatment such as tempering) and leaves the shop as a finished product.

4) The design of a work chain must keep up with the fast progress of modern technology that continuously improves manufacturing tools and processes. Yet changes in one link of a chain will inevitably have a certain effect on the structure of the whole chain.

Data on the issue of technology-related patents in the USA serve to illustrate this point. (The figures are the average number per year).

1880-1890................................19, 600

1890-1900 22,100

1900-1910 35,000

5) Sound production cooperation among detail workers requires a sound structure of the production chain as well as *good organization of the workflow along this chain.* The latter task is just as daunting as the former. At advanced modern factories there is no need to leave the workplace – the raw material comes to the worker and leaves the worker in a steady and well calculated flow like blood in the circulatory system.

"The packing shop of a major American trading company has an inspector who makes sure that the whole batch of goods that arrives every hour is packed 3 to 5 minutes before the set time. The system works in such a way that whatever is not packed should not delay the handling of the next batch. The core packing staff cannot delay the processing of the next batch if the previous one is not finished; the outstanding job is done by a special team."

The Ford Motor Company maintains uninterrupted production by means of an internal transportation system that constantly moves the parts to be machined along the shortest routes possible. These railways and chutes free up the floor area, reduce the number of personnel needed to carry the products, and spare workers from unnecessary motions that, according to estimates by Ford engineers, may take up to a half of the working time. The assembly process is split into minute operations performed by the worker as the car frame passes by; occasionally the worker would make a step aside and promptly return to his basic position.

6) Finally, we should not forget that old-time industrial managers such as engineers and "loner" type administrators have a mentality that largely prevents them from designing the factory as an integrated automatic mechanism whose every movement should be rigorously calculated as a specific component of the entire system. Also, the traditional industrial administration system is manifestly unfit for this goal.

Hence *the current organizational crisis* and the emergence of a special profession of an administrator and organizer that has brought about the theoretical and practical NOT movement.   It is a crisis of individualism and traditionalism in work habits, a crisis of skills and attitudes of *an isolated worker at the essentially collective modern manufacturing company.*

5.   *Picture of a crisis-type organization*

Let us provide a few vivid illustrations to this organizational crisis, as well as the demise of skills and techniques of an isolated worker in today's Russian industry.

"The general organization of factories left much to be desired. Calculations were sometimes left unfinished and sometimes were outright wrong. One of the greatest vulnerabilities was the division of management functions. The director of a large machine-building plant with dozens of shops was usually bogged down in trivial day-to-day problems and had neither support staff nor time to coordinate the operations of individual shops and prepare development plans, which, given the current structure of the factory, was not an easy job. Factory management was based on (personal) contacts among employees, their (personal) memory and business skills. The detailed structure of departments was inevitably just as backward as that of the factory at large. Technological and administrative functions were often intertwined, a clear-cut system was lacking, and operations were in many cases based on habits, traditions and (personal) relations." (Grinevetsky, "Post-War prospects of the Russian industry").

"If we visit the director's office, we shall almost inevitably see it crowded with employees who are complaining that they have spent several days waiting for a one-minute talk with the director to discuss a problem that frustrates their work. He is either absent, busy, or in a hurry."

"A letter to management may go unanswered for a week or two. If you drop by to inquire what was done about your problem, you'll see people hustling around and looking for your letter; it will turn out that it was forwarded to some department, and people will start recalling which department that was and ask various departments whether they received it."

"The manager of the mechanical shop is being torn apart. Foremen want drawings needed to give assignments to workers; materials have to be ordered from suppliers and storage; something broke down somewhere and has to be fixed; at the same time, new drawings arrive from the technology office – but he hardly has any time to look at them; orders to the casting shop, the forgery and the supply department are hastily written; no time to identify parts to be made as a priority; workers are waiting for assignments; the manager checks which parts have to be manufactured next and starts inquiring whether the blanks that correspond to the drawings have arrived yet. A sudden telephone call or a note summons him to the director for an unscheduled meeting since the director has no daily schedule at all. The foremen have either to waste time waiting or make their own decisions. If the office operates in such a chaotic way, what happens at the workplace?"

"A worker who has finished his task stops the machine and looks for the foreman to have his job accepted and get a new task; the foreman had no time to prepare the task and has to go to the shop manager's office to get drawings. The worker is waiting, his machine is idle. Once the task is given, he has to find the blank in the shop or the storage room. The machine is still idle. It turns out that for this task one needs some special support or braces that have to be found somewhere or borrowed from fellow workers (who are thus distracted from work); sometimes a crane is needed or help with mounting the blank, that's a new hassle; the machine is still idle. Finally, the blank is mounted and secured, but the cutting tool has to be honed – and the machine is still idle."

"Let us come to the foundry in the morning. A well-paid molder has found a heap of dirt from yesterday's work at his workplace. He has to level the dirt, remove whatever brackets, hooks and nails it may contain, add some dry sand (that has to be fetched from somewhere), and find the foreman to get his task and a model. The model is not always available on the spot and has to be retrieved from the model department or the storage room; sometimes it may be broken and has to be fixed. Then the worker has to find a foundry flask (occasionally, the right size would be unavailable and a larger flask has to be used, which is not good for casting). He has then to select the entire set of accessories and wait for its delivery. Brackets, hooks and chaplets have to be retrieved from the storage room. To turn the flask upside down the molder waits for the crane or has to find general help. If cores are needed, he has to go to the core unit; sometimes they are not ready or have not dried, so more time is wasted. In any ship-building or bridge construction shop we would inevitably hear that some men did not report to work because materials had not been delivered."

In fact, metallurgical works would deliver heavy structural stock or large shipments of identical parts relatively fast, since such orders help them meet their output target. Smaller parts or those ordered in limited numbers are of little interest to the supplier, so he would procrastinate as long as possible. Designers, especially in shipbuilding or bridge construction, endeavor to save on weight by designing custom parts and paying no attention to the fact that a single assembly would contain dozens of unique parts that would be on the list of products available but would be hard to get hold of in practice. Sometimes, in order to avoid delays, workers cut off segments of larger angle bars or sheets delivered for a future job; expensive material is therefore wasted and later the parts have to be reordered and will possibly arrive late.

In the assembly shop people will inevitably complain they had to delay work for lack of necessary parts, usually small ones.

Indeed, the output of each individual shop is measured by weight, which makes little sense, since jobs may be very different. Workers often get bonuses for producing extra weight. Accordingly, shops do their best to make larger parts of all the orders first, while smaller ones are delivered later, so assembly is delayed."

"Now the main office of the factory, where all these details of work on each order are not known, receives a telegram from the client who complains that work is behind schedule, begs to work faster and asks when the order will be delivered. A new round of hassle starts. The assembly shop, the mechanical shop, the foundry, the forgery and the model shop blame each other. The order is given top priority while others are put aside. An unfinished part in the machine is replaced by a new one. Pressure is put on assembly workers to work faster; they are doing a sloppy job so once the order is delivered, some parts are ill-fitting and some small things are not finished or just forgotten."

"The cost of a finished or unfinished product can be found out only by interviewing foremen, timekeepers and office clerks from various departments making samplings. These calculations are slow and have a large margin of error. The cost, however, is needed to find the price for a new order, ask for a payment due or a new loan.

This is the picture of a factory that has no systematic organization."

In this clear and colorful sketch Kanegisser shows all the elements of a modern haphazard manufacturing facility. It is fully evident that such an organization cannot be sustainable.

This organization is wasteful. It may be equipped with advanced machinery but manufacturing costs would inevitably be too high. It cannot take full advantage of its machines. It wastes an enormous amount of raw materials, human effort and energy. While caring for *technology* only, it completely ignores the principles of sound *organization.* The technological side of manufacturing may be well planned, calculated and scientifically designed. The organizational side, however, is chaotic, archaic and wasteful.

To avoid losing the battle with competition, it has to meet the rigorous condition of industrialism, i.e., *to realize the collective (cooperative) nature of machine production and overcome the organizational crisis.*

6.   *Organizational crisis in modern industry*

We have already noted above that today's transition-type organization of industry is wasteful and counterproductive. There is more to this problem, however, than mere economics. There is a far more significant underlying process, the profound organizational crisis of industrial (and, more generally, any other work-related) collectives in the industrial society. This crisis manifests in numerous ways; essentially, *a modern large collective-labor organization cannot be managed using obsolete methods based on traditionalism and individualism, a legacy of small-scale industry.* As we shall see below, the management system described by Kanegisser is, in fact, a typical individualist and authoritarian organization of a small shop that is applied to a factory whose very size, objectives and inherent structure (cooperative-labor, according to Marx) call for a dramatically different kind of management. The organizational crisis, therefore, is the sharp contradiction between the management system in use and the volume and nature of operations.

Chapter III. The Staff Principle in Large-scale Industry

1. Management at small vs. large enterprises

Small factories are managed entirely on a *personal or individual basis.* Their operations and overall success depend on factors such as intuition, undocumented traditions, personal discretion and the direct influence of the chief executive officer as opposed to impartial, detailed and precise calculations, rigorous planning and strict organization. A degree of planning and calculating in this case may be applied to a *certain* operation or a *group* of operations rather than to the work process as a whole. More or less precise estimates may be prepared in connection with a specific purchase or a specific order. However, a small business owner would hardly ever plan his purchases well in advance, ponder over prospective work methodologies, or think about the chain of work and the manufacturing flow. In fact, such thoughts are inherently alien to such a manager because he operates on *personal discretion* and issues orders at the moment he feels something is needed.

A large factory is in a different situation. Its very survival in a competitive environment critically depends on comprehensive and meticulous *accounting,* a careful preliminary design of all economic activities, a detailed and thoroughly considered *long-term work plan,* strict work procedures that Americans and Englishmen call "a work routine" without any negative connotations and what we could more appropriately call *the automatism of collective labor.* A direct *personal order* and, to an even greater extent, *personal discretion* at such a factory is of limited relevance. Personal discretion gives way to rigorous *accounting, planning and detailed design* as the only way to manage hundreds and thousands of detail workers and the manufacturing flow that passes through their hands. In fact, these rules apply to any large entity. No personal discretion or individual order would make sense, say, in today's *Tsentrosoyuz* [The Central Union of Consumer Cooperatives – Translator's note], where the processing of a wholesale order requires 262 operations and involves a work chain of 160 people, or at any ministry, where papers pass through the hands of 10 to 15 isolated partial workers.

2. Management in a transition-type organization

How can we describe management at a transition-type organization described by Grinevetskiy and Kanegisser? A close look at the picture presented by these authors shows that every stage of production as well as the entire system is managed on a personal basis. Because of inertia, people try to run a large and complex enterprise much like a small business owner runs his shop, i.e., based on direct personal impressions and impacts. This "personal management regime" by everybody from a foreman to the director has the following features:

1. Direct personal control (through orders and follow-up) by a supervisor on his subordinates concerning any emerging problem.

2. Orders are based on personal opinions.

3. Managers exercise personal discretion in handling any specific issue.

4. Managers take care of any issue that comes to their attention (universalism of management).

These salient features of the personal management regime may be described in a less benevolent way by indicating that such a system has

1) No impartial, precise and systematic accounting for every stage of manufacturing;

2) No preliminary calculations and no development of the most efficient work techniques;

3) No meticulous long-term work plan based on objective calculations.

Because of these three deficiencies, personal discretion becomes the central factor of management.

4) No sound and strict internal work regulations in place;

5) (a) No clear division of responsibilities among white-collar staff; (b) no clear-cut division of labor by function.

This is why management has to get involved in the resolution of every issue that comes by (universalism of management).

6) No detailed planning or calculation of workflow processes, no conscious design of the work chain.

All these six deficiencies lead to discretion, universalism and involvement in every specific issue as the key features of personal management.

This is the way a small business owner works.

Because of inertia, however, people try to use the same practices in the management of large and complex groups of workers. The fact that larger-scale operations require a long chain of managers at various levels makes no difference. Each manager mimics a small business owner within the area of his own responsibility, which is also not clearly separated from adjacent areas, and the chief manager follows suit with regard to the enterprise as a whole. Numerous factories, plants, and agencies are often run as a mechanical aggregate of many small shops, each operated by a single owner. Grinevetskiy notes that «many Russian factories with 5 to 10 thousand employees were, in fact, an uncoordinated combination of individual shops held together by common administration rather than proper design."

This individualistic and autocratic style of management is currently in crisis. It proved to be incapable of organizing and controlling large and complex groups of workers. Professional administrators who emerged in the 1890s and started the scientific and practical NOT movement to struggle with individualism, traditionalism, and autocracy in today's management of such groups.

3. Management in the modern army

Since this individualistic type of management was found to be inadequate for directing complex large-scale actions rather long ago, a quest started for alternative management techniques, especially in the army. Being the earliest form of the organization designed for concerted action, the army is also vitally important to the state and critically needs the utmost degree of coordination among various units. For these reasons, the army was the first organization to embark on the path to alternative management that would be more appropriate for large-scale activities. Note that this process was not thwarted even by the fact that military commanders until recently were recruited mostly from the backward class of noble land owners with a rather conservative mentality.

We shall leave aside an intriguing new issue of relations between civil, industrial and military administration. However, let us mention some typical progressive features of military administration that have emerged as a result of concentrated management of large groups of people.

1. *Impartial accountability and advance planning* are applied to all principal aspects of military life such as mobilization, manning, operations, drills, and logistics.

2. *Command functions are separated from accounting and planning.*

Accounting and planning are delegated to special *staff departments* that thoroughly plan each operation before it is executed under an order from the commander.

In contrast to the transition-type factory manager who is overwhelmed with thousands of specific petty problems and therefore can hardly direct the enterprise as a whole, the army commander delegates all the work on detailed accounting, calculations, preparation and execution of an operation to others, while concentrating on strategic issues pertaining to consistent and sound performance of his organization.

It is this detailed and well calculated preliminary work at the staff that makes it possible to guide million-strong armies stretched along front lines that are thousands of miles long, to organize concerted firing by 2800 artillery units with 10,000 guns, immediately followed by an assault of several hundred infantry divisions, as was the case during the World War.

3. Record-keeping and planning alone by staff officers are not enough to execute such large-scale operations. Of equal importance is the strict and meticulous work routine that we would rather call *collective work automatism in an organization,* where the authority of a manager over his coworkers is somewhat limited.

4. Rational and truly Taylor-style training of servicemen to perform a certain range of basic actions almost automatically.

5. A powerful education campaign to foster ownership among servicemen, their keen interest in the successes and failures of the organization. Active pressure is put on servicemen to make them feel like genuine members of the army.

6. Personnel selection based on scientific medical data and, in certain key cases, psychotechnics **(7)**.

7. The principles of collective organization and collective interactions as applied to army management, education, strategy, and tactics have been meticulously studied. The results are about to be formalized as a true sociology of collective organization and interactions.

4. *The staff and management*

With the spontaneous concentration of management in the industrial society, these progressive features of large-scale collective labor organizations are currently spreading to factories. As we have already said, in this chapter we shall be dealing only with accounting and planning aspects of management at large enterprises, or, in other words, the role of the staff.

Again, while the size of production units has been growing fast, their internal organization remained archaic for a long time. The cooperative nature of production was ignored. Factories were run as small shops and management relied on personal opinions and discretion, direct personal orders, supervision, and involvement in all specific petty issues by the manager (universalism) that came to his attention. The factory could be adding new shops, divisions, and departments, hiring more workers and buying more machinery, business could be growing but management philosophy hardly ever changed. What was expanding and swelling was the hierarchy of intermediate bosses who, although on a varying scale, performed the same function of issuing "personal orders" and directly supervising subordinates at their own discretion.

However, with the growing scale of production, the need to improve work techniques and the increasing complexity of issues to be addressed by management, the principles of organization started changing in a major way, primarily in the following directions:

1) A special staff center is set up under the head office to deal with objective accounting, control and detailed planning;

2) The function of direct management at the smallest executive unit level (a gang at a factory or a subdivision of an agency) loses its "personal" character;

The old management chain (*specific issue – personal impression of the manager – personal discretion of the manager – order – execution – follow-up)* has proven to be too crude, wasteful, and arbitrary. Dramatic changes are needed.

First of all, management must become an automatic process. In order to reach this goal:

1) *General management* as a strategic function *is separated from administration* of routine matters;

2) The direct internal administration is moved as close as possible to operations units to relieve senior management. As Field Marshal Moltke **(8)** put it: *"A commander should give orders that concern only the issues that his subordinate cannot handle himself".*

These reforms have an immediate effect on the first and the last member of the above formula, i.e., "specific issues" and "follow-up". The flow of specific issues and responses goes to the bottom of the hierarchy, i.e., these are dealt with directly by junior personnel who are accountable on these matters to senior operations management. The director of the factory (or agency) receives work reports and follow-up information that cover the whole range of problems faced by the organization and ways to address these issues.

Some of the problems included in these reports may draw the director's attention as being new or particularly complicated.

The second dramatic change in management mechanisms concerns the middle members of the formula, i.e., *the means of addressing problems.*

The establishment of a staff to deal with accounting, project design and planning destroys the foundations of the autocratic regime such as personal impressions and personal discretion.

The new system encourages the director who faces a new or a particularly complicated issue to charge the staff with addressing the problem rather than rely on his own impressions and discretion. Staff officers consequently suggest a range of detailed options based on reliable information and scientific knowledge. To make such options available is the main objective of the staff's creative work. Even when a way to address the problem is directly proposed by others, the staff, as the intellectual center of the agency, must still explore alternative options. As Schellendorf said, *"a General Staff officer can consider himself right only if he asks for an appropriate order from the commanding officer but the request is denied."* Suggesting an alternative solution is both the privilege and the direct responsibility of a staff.

Once endorsed by the director, the option becomes a directive that is sent to administration for execution according to an enclosed instruction prepared by the staff.

Therefore, the establishment of a staff fundamentally changes the nature of management by destroying the personal or individualistic attitude.

1) The staff principle teaches the senior manager to think in organizational terms. Once endorsed by the director, the option becomes a directive that is sent to administration for execution according to an enclosed instruction prepared by the staff.

Therefore, the establishment of a staff fundamentally changes the nature of management by destroying the personal or individualistic attitude.

1) The staff principle teaches the senior manager to think in organizational terms. The endless chaotic array of specific problems and specific actors that fills his mind under the old system is now replaced with an orderly chain of emerging tasks that are fulfilled by an impersonal team.

2) Personal and universal discretion gives way to advance planning based on objective data and specialized scientific knowledge.

3) Administration enjoys considerable freedom and right of initiative when addressing the problems they are charged with. Relations between employees are not affected by the personal management regime anymore. They become more "objective" and, as we shall see in the next chapter, tend to foster the team spirit.

3) Administration enjoys considerable freedom and right of initiative when addressing the problems they are charged with. Relations between employees are not affected by the personal management regime anymore. They become more "objective" and, as we shall see in the next chapter, tend to foster the team spirit.

5. *Expansion of the staff principle to manufacturing*

The staff principle in manufacturing is not something entirely new. It has been gradually and painlessly permeating industrial organizations to become deeply rooted in technology-related aspects of their operations

Staff-type bodies dealing with research, development, follow-up, and training to fulfill *specific manufacturing tasks* have been established in large companies as special laboratories or research and development units. Today's manufacturing would be incapable of continuous technological breakthroughs without large and sophisticated R&D departments such as those operated by General Electric in New

York (127 engineers and 225 technicians), Westinghouse (132 engineers) or Western Electric Company (825 employees). These *technological staffs* support state-of-the art manufacturing at a minimum cost by means of meticulous research and planning.

At the First International NOT Congress in Prague in 1924 **(9)** Holland presented some data on the operation of R&D units in the USA. That country has 578 industrial research laboratories that cost 150 million dollars a year to run.

Here is an example from a machine-building factory to illustrate how a R&D department operates.

"The R&D department is charged with adapting an available machine to some special processing task. The engineers start an in-depth study of this machine, trying to take as much advantage of the existing mechanism as possible.

Once the new design is essentially ready, a prototype is made. It is carefully studied by a special engineer who checks all the details of the design and works on enhancing the model so as to save on materials and reach a maximum efficiency.

After this work is successfully finished, the head office issues an order to start commercial production, and engineers at R&D start preparing drafts and workshop drawings to be used by manufacturing departments."

This is how the technological (engineering) staff operates at a factory. Such a centralized attitude that has replaced small business manager's personal discretion with research and development based on precise data and scientific methods is the sole way to sustain the rapid progress of today's technology.

On the other hand, as we see from the above considerations, industrialism calls for perfect *organizational techniques as well as for excellent engineering.*

Large-scale manufacturing and complex cooperation among partial workers with their own narrow specialization require more than a good model of a superb product and perfect machines for its production.

"The cooperative character of the labor-process is... a technical necessity dictated by the instrument of labor itself," Marx wrote.

The manufacturing process as cooperation between partial workers and the very organization of collective labor requires no less attention today than pure technology. The new attitude should be based on detailed and precise record-keeping, research and forward planning. No machine can operate outside of the "directly associated labor" system that cannot be managed using traditional individualistic methods like a small business. The mechanism of an organization should be designed as carefully as that of a machine. Accordingly, this requires special staff for record keeping, research, development and strategic management. This is the only way to address the current organizational crisis in large-scale manufacturing.

Indeed, advanced enterprises that manage to survive the perils of transition and overcome the painful organizational crisis establish not only R&D departments but organizational staffs represented by so-called organization and planning (distribution) divisions.

These management staffs are facing the following broad issues:

1. Install the best machines and auxiliary equipment throughout the factory and organize their best possible operation.

2. Design the best workflow patterns and control them on a daily basis in terms of prescribed stages (routes) and times.

3. Organize "directly associated labor" and cooperation among partial workers to form an integrated chain of work.

In the next chapter we shall see that the last task (organization of cooperation among workers) has become so important and so challenging compared to the first two, that post-Taylorist management thinkers believe that it should be handled by a special staff, i.e., the administration division.

The work of the administration division is by no means a transient or an occasional task that can be fulfilled once and

95

for all. It is just as continuous and stressful as that of the engineering staff. First, it covers design, management, and control of the manufacturing flow. Second, it is similar to engineering staff work just because it can never end. Organizational and engineering improvements have no limits.

A yesterday's achievement becomes obsolete today and a burden tomorrow. One has to move on forever in engineering and administration improvement alike.

This is why hard work is needed every single day to ensure the best organization of labor.

The administration division concentrates its efforts on record-keeping, design and development with the following objectives:

1) the best use of raw materials,

2) the best use of machines,

3) the highest product quality,

4) the best work techniques,

5) the fastest work motions,

6) The greatest coherence and regularity of the manufacturing flow;

7) The best structure of the manufacturing chain that consists of partial workers.

6.   The staff principle in a factory shop

Manufacturing as a whole involves complex cooperation among partial workers. This applies to production (where concentration, as we have seen above, has led to deep specialization) as well as to administration. The management of a large factory is also based on complex cooperation among partial workers each of whom performs a distinct partial function.

We have just seen how the general management system has expanded, become more sophisticated and differentiated while gaining more authority and precision.

The apparently simple autocratic mechanism of management (personal impression—personal discretion—order—supervision over the actor) was, in fact, a highly complex process. Now it has disintegrated into a number of processes and differentiated subsystems:

1) senior (general) management,

2) intellectual center for records, comparative analysis, design and planning (the staff),

3) administration (execution and internal regulations).

This differentiation aimed at squeezing out the traditional authoritarian approach has certainly not been limited to senior management. It was bound to permeate the entire enterprise and transform it from top to bottom. This effect could be expected to be even stronger at the bottom, i.e., at the lowest operations level. As it happens, this was indeed the case.

In the smallest production unit the foreman plays the same role as the factory director under the "personal regime" does with regard to the entire enterprise.

The traditional foreman also vividly reflects the traditional authoritarian features of a small workshop owner (universalism, personal impression and discretion, direct personal orders to every worker on every specific occasion, personal supervision over workers themselves rather than their performance).

This petty boss has a number of various nominal functions such as (1) work process planning, (2) control over the maintenance of tools, (3) control over the installation of machines, (4) timely delivery of raw materials and semi-finished articles, (5) quality control, (6) accounting and other paperwork, (7) personnel selection and training, (8) control over order and work discipline and many others.

To perform all these varied tasks a man should possess a combination of personal qualities that simply does not exist in reality. "Even if is such a man is found, - notes Taylor, - you better appoint him factory manager rather than foreman".

This fictional jack-of-all-trades who manages every single issue and every single worker is replaced in today's industry by a real-life group of experts affecting the production chain within the limits of their narrow specialization. Some of them deal with *records and planning*, others with instruction and supervision.

The instructors and supervisors operate on the shop floor:

1) *The work setup instructor* shows the machinists how to set up the job in the machine properly and quickly.

2) *The speed boss* sees that the machine is run at the best speed and that the proper tool is used in a particular way (refeeding speed and cutting depth as indicated on the instruction card) to finish the job in the shortest possible time. His duties start once the job is set up in the machine and end once the machining process is over.

He often has to demonstrate the workmen that the job can indeed be finished in a prescribed time.

3) *The quality inspector* accepts the job.

4) *The maintenance instructor* monitors the status of machines and tools.

The records and the planning part of the unit operate from the planning (distribution) room and deal with the issues that are critical to the new system of organization:

1) *The route clerk* regulates the workflow along the manufacturing chain much like railway traffic. Once the proper clerk defines the entire route for a given job from one machine to another so that the job is finished as fast as possible at a minimum cost, the route manager prepares a daily instruction for workmen and foremen that precisely specifies the order of work. These instructions provide the principal guidance on the distribution of work among machinists.

2) *The instruction card clerk.* While the previous manager is responsible for design and planning of the *order* of the work process, this clerk deals with *the way to perform work operations.* The instruction card is the main instrument for the planning department to describe all the details of work. Such

cards identify general and detailed drawings needed for the job, the job number and the receipt number, special tools and implements, means of setting up the job in the machine, where processing has to start, cutting depth, feeding (advance) speed and the time allotted for each particular operation. It also indicates the pay for a timely job. If needed, the name of the foreman (instructor) for special guidance is mentioned as well. Such instruction cards are prepared by one or several persons from the planning department depending on their complexity. They are the output of the planning department as drawings are the product of the drawing department. A special clerk is charged with (1) transmitting the instruction cards to shops, and (2) providing all the necessary explanations.

3) *The time and pay clerk* enters all the data concerning the time and rate on the instruction cards, controls relevant data inflow and transmits all the necessary information to bookkeepers for recording.

4) While the shop manager's position is not abolished, he *becomes a pure administrator* responsible for a difficult and important job of properly coordinating the efforts of these three groups of personnel (planners, instructors and workmen). We shall discuss this issue later in the current chapter.

This is how the modern manufacturing mechanism operates. As we see, it is vastly different from its historical predecessors.

7.   *Work under staff-based management*

Pearson gives a graphic description of the difference between the old and the new system. "When an order arrives, it is sent to a foreman with an instruction "to make 25 pieces by June 25". The foreman approaches a workman and asks him to do the job by the day after tomorrow.

The foreman, therefore, did some planning. He selected a machinist, defined the time needed for the job and the way to do it.

"Scientific organization is different. Planning is done in a special room where data about each stage of the operation are carefully stored. First, all these stages, as well as the materials and tools required for the operation, are written down on an instruction sheet. Second, the time needed for each stage is calculated with some allowance for possible troubles. Third, the day to start the job is determined so it could be finished by the deadline. Work orders based on these calculations are sent to the warehouse clerk with an instruction to deliver the job at a certain time to a certain machine and a certain workman. These are accompanied by a detailed job description and clear instructions to the machinist."

Another good example comes from a person who happened to observe the functional planning approach on Russian turf. A shipment of expensive modern machines for a large factory has been delivered by steamship. It is accompanied by a large group of American workers. Rumors of their arrival have long been circulating among factory employees, so a large throng comes to meet the ship. The spectators are stunned to see how quickly and efficiently the parts are collected and loaded on carts. "These Americans act like a soccer team," people wonder.

The boxes are unloaded at the factory yard under a canopy. The locals are very curious about the way Americans would cope with installing the heavy machines in factory shops. A day passes, and another one. It appears the Americans do not care. They are just strolling in small groups around the yard, the stairways and the shops where space has been cleared for them. "You bet these softies will make us do their job," some say viciously. However, on the second or third day the Americans, again acting "as a soccer team" transport and install the machines in a mere couple of hours. It turned out that during "the idle period" they were doing precise calculations and planning to install the machines as efficiently as possible.

Let us sum up the typical features of a modern organization.

1. Record-keeping and planning are separated from actual manufacturing, management and administration.

2. A special planning and distribution department is established.

3. A sound system is introduced for functional chains (social labor organization), supply of tools and materials, as well as the progress of jobs down the manufacturing chain.

4. Specialized workers are organized in work chains that take care of the manufacturing flow.

5. Supervisors are clearly divided into functional groups under centralized management; a planning department, a group of instructors and supervisors and a general administration unit are established.

6. The manufacturing process is regulated by the administration with the help of data and plans supplied by the planning department.

7. The entire new system involves incessant research and development to improve work motions, tools, materials and the like.

Chapter IV. Social Organization of a Modern enterprise (agency)

1. *Cooperative nature of an enterprise*

As seen from the previous chapters, the management of large modern enterprises undergoes fundamental changes due to (1) fierce competition that requires consistent improvements (including those in management) to reach the highest efficiency; (2) the increasing size and complexity of enterprises; (3) the *cooperative* nature of labor at large enterprises that absolutely needs coordination and continuity of all manufacturing processes in one fast manufacturing flow.

A modern factory manager, even at the lowest (foreman) level, cannot afford to act like a small business owner, i.e., pretend to be more experienced and knowledgeable than any of his subordinates with respect to any specific problem that comes by. Industrial management now calls for much more attention and analysis. It can no longer rest on *personal discretion,* since modern manufacturing has become too broad and complex, every partial worker is too specialized, and every operation must be too meticulously calculated and planned.

Personal discretion (that is, personal intuition plus undocumented tradition) as an attitude to management has proven to be inadequate in today's industrial environment. This attitude is now being crowded out from management and administration just as it was crowded out from engineering during the XIX century to be replaced by *objective and precise record-keeping, detailed scientific research, advance design, and planning.*

Industrialism has led modern large-scale manufacturing to an organizational crisis caused by the struggle between the unfolding cooperative nature of labor and the restraints imposed on it by the traditional individualistic management (the isolated worker system), a legacy of small business. This crisis has shattered personal discretion as the basis of management and replaced it with the *staff principle* that involves good accounting, research and planning.

However, the current organizational revolution in large-scale manufacturing is much broader. Industrialism evokes the cooperative nature of large-scale manufacturing to assault the personal regime of the "isolated worker" throughout the system. It covers technology as well as *social organization. It affects not only relations among things and those between things and humans but also relations among people involved in the production process.*

In other words, the cooperative nature of a modern large company calls for the strict planning of all the elements of the labor process by partial workers as well as for *the sound organization of people as participants in integrated work cooperation.* While abolishing *personal discretion* as the principle of individualistic management, this revolution also destroys *individualistic micro-management* as well as the opposite pole of this system, i.e., *blind obedience by the worker.*

102

As we have seen above, the simple old formula of "a specific order followed by specific execution" was *the true axis of management* at a small factory from top to bottom. Industrialism offers a far more modern pattern of relations within the collective labor process. Industrialism flatly rejects all the attitudes and skills of an isolated worker. A modern enterprise is organized by means of strict accounting and planning rather than personal discretion. It replaces direct orders and supervision by a corporate work system, rigorous collective labor routines, automatism of collective labor and fostering collective ownership with regard to the production process.

As opposed to the old individualistic authoritarian regime based on personal supervision, this is a *systematic cooperative labor regime,* or, if we may, a *regime of substance.*

Everything in a small workshop is subject to the owner's personal will, discretion and supervision. The worker is expected to look at himself and at his object of labor, so to say, with the owner's eyes. Indeed, the owner is less interested in technological and manufacturing issues (in these matters he relies on previous experience) than in the daily behavior of each specific worker. He is "behind his back" at all times to "urge" the worker. The small business typically prefers personal supervision to control over delivery.

A large industrial enterprise operates in a different way. It rejects direct personal interaction between the manager and the subordinate. The enterprise builds a harmonious system by means of (1) social and technological division of labor, (2) creation of functional teams, (3) orientation of each group towards relations between things and workers, (4) controlling these relations by planning that also applies to social and organizational relations between actors.

The social and technological division of labor has led to the establishment of the following principal groups:

1) general management (strategic tasks),

2) research and planning (specific plans),

3) internal administration and control over orders,

4) operations (execution of orders).

The entire art and the overarching objective of management at a large factory is to provide a clear system of job assignments to each of these groups and subgroups, supply all the necessary instructions and materials to fulfill these assignments, provide as much freedom as possible to the executor, generate and continuously maintain the interest of each group in the best execution of the task – and organize all this into an integrated, smooth and fast manufacturing flow.

Advanced industrial organizations regulate work techniques and the work flow, use objective controls and actively foster ownership with regard to teamwork as well as the operation of the enterprise as a whole. All these policies emphasize rather than suppress the cooperative nature of modern manufacturing.

Therefore, the organizational revolution in industry has evoked the cooperative nature of large-scale production. While consistently applying the accounting and planning principle to the manufacturing process as a whole, it *goes much further by commanding human relations in the manufacturing process and transforming the authoritarian individualistic management style into a fundamentally different system of collective labor cooperation.* This new system is not regulated by "supervision over personnel". Rather, it directly affects production relations ("the objective manufacturing organism of the enterprise") on a planned basis while consistently nurturing *"the spirit of the hive", i.e., the interest in a successful fulfillment of the task by every team and by the entire work collective.*

2. Cooperative labor vs. "isolated worker" skills

The group of professional organizers and administrators behind the organizational revolution and the NOT movement has to wage a fierce daily struggle with the lingering mentality and skills of "the isolated worker" and with the still prevailing "personal management regime". This conflict is sharp and irreconcilable.

As we have seen above, the social roots of the personal management regime have already been undercut by rapid industrial concentration. Nevertheless, they are still fairly strong. The persistent tradition of management created by the previous generation of large industry builders knows only the isolated rather than social worker since it had no experience other than that of running a small business (based on the manager's personality). All those winners of enormous fortunes who founded large-scale industries had an isolated worker mentality, the only option in the petty bourgeois environment where they came from. Moreover, their personal life experience of a tooth-to-nail struggle with everybody by any means to make their progress from the bottom to the heights of capitalist prosperity could only make this mentality even more uncompromising.

To illustrate our observations, here is some information on the past of American billionaires, the founders of the most concentrated industry in the world. The steel king of America, Charles Schwab, "was an errand boy who became a billionaire", the multibillionaire Carnegie started as a bobbin boy at a cotton factory; Henri Rogers, the founder of Standard Oil and later a major copper trust, used to work as a clerk in a colonial goods store; John Kets, a son of a small farmer, used to own "a tiny hardware shop". James McGill, born to a Canadian farmer, worked as a sales clerk and an assistant steamship fireman, the silver king M. Clark, born to a farmer from Pennsylvania, worked as a farmer, miner, salesman, horse dealer and so on.

A similar, though somewhat less conspicuous process took place in continental Europe. Ratenau, an expert on capitalist organization **(10)**, testifies to it from a rather unconventional standpoint: "The former generations, the people of the industrial revolution, could become conquerors on their own. Today, in the time of strong organizations, these people are trying to find successors who would master new management methods, the techniques of staff art that have now become daily practices. Being a product of a dangerous economic experiment, they do not want this experiment to be conducted on others."

Ratenau's idyllic tone aside, let us take note of his competent opinion, that is, (1) economic environment and management techniques in the era of mature industrialism are entirely different from those in the times of early capitalism; (2) these differences essentially correspond to our observations above.

We should not think that the personal regime of the isolated worker belongs only to the top of the capitalist hierarchy. It used to pervade the entire governance system from top to bottom including every link in the management chain.

The isolated worker is a jack-of-all-trades, a universal being, an artisan, and a know-all. His power depends exclusively on his personality. His success rests on stubborn self-assurance and equally stubborn *distrust* in others as either inferior workers or his competitors. These are men of steel who became economic conquerors in the era of emerging large-scale manufacturing. Nowadays, however, when that haphazardly built industry should reach its true potential, such characters are becoming irrelevant. Their philosophy and way of thinking pulverize rather than consolidate. They firmly believe the old saying coined in the early predatory days of trade capitalism, that man is a wolf to man. Such an attitude does not help organize cooperation in modern times. True, it can heap up mountains of dead matter, congregate thousands of people and make them obey somebody else's tough and strong will. At a certain point, however, this willpower fails to properly operate a larger and more complex business. Whenever active interests of multitudes are to be united in a single work flow, the seemingly unrestricted power of the isolated worker turns out to be useless. The isolated worker is incapable of organizing and maintaining mass cooperation. If, thanks to a lucky combination of personal qualities, such a worker manages to organize the cooperation in question, the result would be unsustainable. With a basis so narrow, it would remind of a pyramid put on its apex. All its present and future would depend on a specific personality. Indeed, economists in individualistic France often lament that companies rarely survive their founding owners.

3. *Industrialism rejects the isolated worker*

Industrialism requires a very different style of management. Hundreds and thousands of highly specialized workers cannot cooperate on the narrow foundation of individualism and blind obedience of many to one or a few. We have seen above that this is not feasible for technological reasons. Social and psychological reasons also play a role, however. Industrialism wakes up the masses. Every single person from those hundreds and thousands that do a common job of assembling products at a single site loudly claims that he is an active human being rather than just a passive element of the organization. What happens now to modern manufacturing is similar to processes that once occurred in the army, also an organization created for mass action. The former mercenary refuses to remain a thoughtless instrument used to reach goals that are alien to him. He feels a citizen of his country and wants be a citizen of the army. Just like a modern army, a modern factory – where industrialism has brought to life its cooperative labor nature -- can no longer be managed just by means of blunt force and monetary remuneration for technological, psychological and social reasons.

A worker wants to be a citizen of an industrial organization, a building block of civil society.

A modern organizer of labor cooperation is a man of entirely different skills, talents and expertise. His style contrasts that of his predecessor. What he relies on is good *organization* rather than exceptional and universal managers. *Organization* is probably the motto of the epoch of mature industrialism that best reflects the release and liberation of the cooperative labor character of large-scale manufacturing.

"No great man can (with the old system of personal management) hope to compete with a number of ordinary men who have been properly organized so as efficiently to cooperate," –Taylor correctly notes.

Moeller, an engineer, testifies that the leading principle of a modern economic organization is the desire to liberate manufacturing from personal management, and create a structure in which the production process occurs, so to say, mechanically in order to avoid a situation when a specific worker becomes personally indispensable because of his (unique) experience or excellent memory.

The defeat of the personal principle and the motto of "organization" as a firm demand of our times is obvious and unquestionable even to American businessmen. Clarence Wooley, President of American Radiator Company of New York, claims the following. "Industrial organizations have passed the isolated worker stage. The factory is too large, the interests associated with it are too diverse. A single person can no longer hold a company together by means of his work effort or capital. The (primary) unit of a modern enterprise is a corporation, that is, financial resources, the intellectual and physical energy of numerous people united to reach a common goal."

New unconventional attitudes are invading the economy of today. The world that used to value things in very tangible dollars, kilograms, and horsepowers and so on comes to appreciate the enormous and probably overarching value of a very special phenomenon, i.e., well-coordinated *social and labor organization of people for production.*

This is what Taylor has to say on this subject. "Almost all of the directors of manufacturing companies appreciate the economy of a thoroughly modern, up-to-date, and efficient plant, and are willing to pay for it." *Very few of them, however, realize that the best organization, whatever its cost may be, is in many cases even more important than the plant; nor do they clearly realize that no kind of an efficient organization can be built up without spending money.* The spending of money for good machinery appeals to them because they can see machines after they are bought; but putting money into anything so invisible, intangible and to the average man so indefinite, as an organization seems almost like throwing it away. There is no question that when the work to be done is at all complicated, a good organization with a poor plant will give better results than the best plant with a poor organization. One of the most successful manufacturers in this country was asked recently by a number of financiers whether he thought that the difference between one style of organization and another amounted to providing the company had an up-to-date property located. His answer was: "If I had to choose now between abandoning my present organization and burning down all of my plants which have cost me millions, I should choose the latter. My plants could be rebuilt in a short while with borrowed money, but I could hardly replace my organization in a generation."

4. *Administration is a social activity*

In Taylor's system, the planning department was responsible for the organization of machinery and logistics as well as for that of human resources.

During the post-Taylor era of management reforms in large-scale manufacturing, however, it has become clear that the organization of human resources is so important and difficult that it needs a special treatment.

The NOT (scientific management of labor) movement has differentiated. A stand-alone discipline of scientific administration has emerged to deal with issues of a sound social organization.

In practice, industrial development has given rise to a new system with a distinct administrative function for *internal control of work and relations among personnel.* This system opposes the traditions and skills of the "lone manager", and its special administrative staff addresses problems discussed below.

Rather than being an engineer or technician, the modern organizer and administrator is primarily a social builder, a unifier, and director of human wills. Human resources are much more important to him than machinery.

"The administrator, - Denning says, - is predominantly a regulator and coordinator of human activities rather than a technician dealing with the transformation of dead matter".

"The modern administrator, - Webb writes **(11)**, - belongs to intellectual workers exactly like a lawyer, a doctor, or an engineer. His basic function is not to purchase or sell products or introduce new technologies. His unique professional activity is to organize people, i.e., create groups of workers and guide their activities to ensure the most efficient (labor) cooperation that helps reach the organization's common goals."

O. Tead **(12)** and H. Metcalf define personnel administration as "the direction and coordination of the human relations of any organization with a view to getting the maximum necessary production with a minimum of effort and friction, and with a proper regard for the genuine well-being of the workers."

The modern administrator is largely a social technician or engineer (depending on his rank in the system), a constructor of human relations. The higher his office, the larger the number of subordinates he unites and guides, the larger is the proportion of administrative activities in his work vs. technological or engineering activities.

A good illustration to this point may be found in the following tables published by Henri Fayol, the leader of the French school of experimental administration.

The same applies to factory managers and politicians.

		Administration	Technical
1.	Workman	5%	85%
2.	Foreman	16	80
3.	Superintendent	25	45
4.	Head of division	30	30
5.	Head of department	35	30
6.	Manager	40	15

		Administration	Technical
1.	Small factory	15%	40%
2.	Mid-size	30	25

| 3. | Very large | 50 | 10 |
| 4. | Huge state-owned company | 60 | 6 |

However approximate and relative Fayol's calculations may be, we should note that he is likely to underestimate the proportion of administrative duties among other functions rather than to overestimate it. Indeed, this table is based on the traditional system of factory management that is not differentiated and has no permanent staff unit.

Therefore the proportion of administrative functions must certainly be higher than Fayol claims.

As a curious coincidence, Marshall quotes an engineer working as a general manager of a large machine-building plant, who also claims that the proportion of his technical (technology-related) duties does not exceed 15% of his total workload.

Therefore, the demise of the Universalist principle in management resulted in the emergence of a special *administrative function* as *a unique social profession aimed at appropriately uniting and guiding collective work efforts.*

5. Transformation of the modern foreman

As we have seen above, a foreman in a traditional individualistic management system was nominally charged with a broad range of universal responsibilities. At that point we also quoted Taylor who said that a man with such abilities hardly exists in nature and even if he could be found, against all odds, he should better be appointed general manager.

Chambonnaud quotes an instruction for foremen at a well-known factory in Paris. According to this document, a foreman must be an example of good behavior. He must be the first one to report to work and the last one to leave; he must be polite and tactful with workers; he must be fully impartial as a supervisor; record those who are late or missing; handle conflicts and incidents in a peaceful and patient manner; make sure all payments are correct; report all workers' claims to management; assume fellow foremen's duties if they are absent; prevent workers from taking tools and materials from other shops; make sure workers do not procrastinate and are busy at all times; check raw materials and test them before processing; make sure workers always have a proper supply of tools; ensure that the shop is always clean; make sure that every worker has a task for at least another day of work. He must be a man of initiative. He must also keep track of inventory and monitor how workers handle machines, especially those that would require lengthy repairs if broken. He must encourage technological innovations and foster workers' interest in such innovations. Also, a foreman must fill about a dozen various reports on a daily basis.

These are the numerous duties to be performed and qualities to be possessed by a foreman. His monitoring and management responsibilities cover virtually everything in his shop. The entire work order rests on his personality, every specific motion needs his involvement, his personal order, and supervision. At the same time, it is fairly obvious that with such a complex workload the foreman's orders could only be based on general and superficial discretion.

Personal discretion and personal orders on every specific issue faced by every member of the gang foster a peculiar style of relations between the supervisor and the worker. The supervisor is typically an isolated worker who "has made his way to the top". He is sure of his supremacy over others, he is meddling with everything and incapable of finishing any task despite his good faith. In fact, such a supervisor simply micromanages his workers in an effort to squeeze as much sweat as possible out of them. All this affects his personal character: Overwhelmed with scores of requests, immersed in disjointed activities and suffering from open or hidden antagonism with fellow workers, he becomes permanently bitter and nervous.

It is obvious that under these conditions we can hardly talk seriously about true guidance and meaningful leadership by this "universal" or "well rounded", as Americans put it, foreman. Individualist management at a large factory (based on universal discretion, direct orders to each specific worker and handling each specific problem faced by this worker) proves irrelevant even at this lowest step of the administrative ladder.

Industrial development leads to a revolution in a shop by dramatically changing work and management techniques. The single "universal" foreman turns into several narrow experts. As we have seen above, work planning, rate calculations and tasks have moved to the planning department. Instruction cards and orders based on objective observations and calculations now determine the workflow in the shop, the processing techniques for each job, the rate, the size of the task, delivery of raw materials and tools.

Instructions concerning work setup, work techniques, repair and quality control are now regarded as special functions distinct from those of the foreman.

Every universal "well rounded" master is now split into several narrow specialists. Work schemes and plans are developed to integrate all these functions into a powerful automatic mechanism of collective labor. It could seem that the foreman becomes unnecessary and his position should be simply abolished.

Nothing could be farther from the truth, however. While all the *technical* functions of the universal foreman have dissipated among various narrow specialists, the glue that was binding them together, i.e., the *administrative work,* has not been replaced.

A shop is a mechanism where all partial functions are delegated to partial experts. Even the most partial of experts, however, is still a human being. This mechanism, accordingly, has a social nature that follows its own logic. No precise planning of the production process, no ideal regulation of responsibilities or the best mechanical control of the manufacturing flow can create an efficient organization. The automatism of social labor cannot be fostered against people's will or even in the absence of such will. A social labor system created against such will or in its absence would be lifeless and devoid of energy. It would be bound to break down along seams since whenever good collaboration is needed, it would be ruined by heavy friction between parts of the system. This is why it is required that an administrator possess a special function of promoting collaboration and enthusiasm aimed at reaching a common goal.

Industrialism wants the foreman to be a pure administrator, a social worker rather than a universal expert. Accordingly, skills expected from a foreman in a modern organization have changed dramatically.

He is supposed to be a leader rather than a gifted technician. He need not be an expert in various work processes or a tough supervisor like the one in the old-type authoritarian organization. He also need not be an expert in advance planning, calculations, training or quality control. All these functions are already delegated to a complex automatic work collective. His job is to kindle team spirit, foster collective enthusiasm, and understanding of work, achieve conscious coordination among numerous people, evoke collective energy and drive the steam engine of the organization along the set track of manufacturing regulations.

"Leadership qualities are more important for a foreman-to-be than technical knowledge. As Tead observes, "the foreman, therefore, should be the man in the department who is most respected as a leader, who is regarded as the coordinator of the efforts of his associates and the guiding mind of the numerous activities in his room. [...] His main task is to foster human relations and attitudes to work that would make manufacturing a success. His true job is that of a psychologist. So the main quality of a candidate is the ability to handle people."

Denning makes another step forward and suggests that candidates for the position of a foreman ought to be elected.

6. Evolution of management staff

We have just seen that industrial development deals a crushing blow to the "isolated worker" at the bottom level of the administrative ladder. The nature of his work has changed as radically as his requisite skills and qualities. There is every reason to assume that changes in management at the top of this ladder, where the entire complex and cumbersome production mechanism is regulated, would be even more startling. In fact, this is exactly the case.

The isolated worker who always knows best, manages best, and wants to meddle with everything around him has been seriously restrained for a long time now. Anxious to hold the reins of a multitude of carts he is in charge of, to make personal decisions on thousands of specific issues that emerge every day in the vast field of his business, sooner or later he would inevitably see that these ambitions cannot materialize in the environment of a huge organization based on partial specialization, if only for physical reasons.

A temporary solution (used probably by all organizations during their early growth period) was to set up *a personal management group* with rather undifferentiated functions that consisted of close assistants and trusted colleagues. People, however, were driven into such groups by high salaries or recruited due to their ties with the general manager. Pretty soon it became evident that this mechanism did not work. The next idea, that is still valid for some relatively backward organizations, was to use the so called 100% complementarity principle.

With some modifications this principle can be of use in advanced organizations as well. We are not talking about complementary knowledge, *the sum of skills* that is fairly constant for all types of organizations and all positions, but about *personal characters* of managers. In this sense the management team must indeed be a complementary "well rounded" mix, and the principle is still valid.

The expansion of the management team, however, failed to solve the problem. The team was still spending all its time and energy on addressing specific problems and therefore lost the idea of the enterprise as a whole. Also, each specific problem at a modern organization required so much time for careful calculations and analysis, that the team had no chance to perform a steady and regular leadership function.

Further evolution of management leads to the following:

1) Permanent and clear division of labor is established in the management team along technical lines.

Separate permanent positions are introduced to deal with

1) technical issues,

2) manufacturing,

3) administration,

4) commerce,

a) sales,

b) purchases.

2) The management function is split into

1) general (strategic management,)

2) internal administration,

3) planning (the staff),

3) Senior management is gradually relieved of specific routine tasks, while more independence is granted to lower management.

This process has the following features:

a)   Orders   become   less   authoritarian.   An intermediate element is added to the old formula of an order followed by execution, i.e., a discussion between the manager and the subordinate on various ways to do the job;

b)   Workers at the same level have regular meetings to help them form an independent team;

c)   Same-level administrators enjoy the right to consult with each other and inform their superiors after the fact.

This stage in the development of rational management was described by Fayol in his theory of experimental administration.

The above-described current stage in the development of management completely breaks up with the individualistic and authoritarian tradition. It has the following basic features:

1. The *staff principle* (advance planning, design and control) is consistently applied;

2. The planning principle spreads throughout the manufacturing process, all management is centralized.

These ideas were fully developed by American engineers' NOT movement late in the 19th century. Finally, the most recent post-Taylor additions to these principles were

3. Administration, as opposed to technical management, becomes a special function of *social organization* at the enterprise and current control over production processes.

As a result, we arrive at the following scheme of division of labor:

A – management group (determinative group) defines economic, financial, production, and other *policies, issues directives* and controls their execution;

B – *general management* is responsible for (1) internal organization issues, (2) general current management based on supervision and control in accordance with appropriate directives;

C – the *staff* is responsible for planning and control. It is supported by a group of *consultants;*

D –*administration* deals with current management and coordination of production processes;

E – office assistants;

F – manufacturing personnel.

Therefore, the management function, once simple and concentrated in the hands of a few, has expanded vastly. Management became the same kind of cooperation among partial workers as production itself.

Chapter V. Administration as a Tool for Building and Regulating the Corporate Social System

1. Fundamentals of administration

These are the fundamentals of good administration:

1. A modern enterprise should be organized as an integral whole based on advance analysis and planning for each of its closely associated components;

2. The enterprise should keep up with technological progress and new ideas in management and continuously work to increase its overall efficiency.

3. A modern enterprise should have an appropriate system of social organization. The authoritarian and individualistic management style, the legacy of small business and early industrialism, must be eliminated. A situation when the general manager acts as the most competent expert with regard to every partial worker is now unthinkable. Industrialism converts this formula to a rather paradoxical opposite: The general manager may now be less technically competent than the groups he manages and guides.

4. Accordingly, the entire administration system is revamped to become more consistent and take advantage of collective labor automatism (by encouraging rather them suppressing the cooperative nature of manufacturing). This means

a) objective supervision and control over orders and execution of tasks,

b) a structure that generates work impulses inside the system,

c) social work aimed at turning personnel into a true team and encouraging ownership.

5. Industrialism has the following effects on administration:

a) administration is separated from purely technical work. The administrator is an expert who guides other experts of varying skills by means of objective supervision and methods of social psychology rather than interferes with their special work;

b) administration, as a distinct technical activity concerned with internal guidance of collective labor, is separated from general management that is responsible for setting objectives and exercising general control.

2. Administration is vastly different from management

With any enterprise, one should distinguish between the internal structure and external relations. It is clear that the former serves the objectives of the latter. The internal structure must be sufficiently flexible to perform precisely the functions that are needed by external relations. Such a structure is not easy to establish. It requires the division of management personnel. Senior management deals with the analysis of changes in the external environment. The other group (which reports to the first one) takes care of the organization itself and its structure and sets it in motion according to instructions. The senior management deals with ever-changing and sophisticated data from the heterogeneous and perilous environment. Precise calculations and rigid planning are less important here than fast decision-making and lucky intuition. Administrators, on the hand, are facing a reasonably stable and enclosed situation, a permanent set of facts and data, and therefore should base their work on accurate calculations, precise knowledge, and clear action plans.

In the military science, these two types of management are referred to as strategic and tactical management. In the economy, they are distinguished as policy-making (meaning financial, social and other policies) and administration.

Strategists give general orders to tactical units and exercise supreme control over execution. The tactical unit should be as flexible as possible to fulfill any general order in the best technical way. Likewise, economic policy-makers give general directives to be followed by the administration that should always stand ready, in terms of both technology and organization.

Therefore, administration is essentially a *technology* for the construction and maintenance of a collective labor system that is entirely different from senior management activities that set goals and provide strategic guidance.

3. Administration is fundamentally different from technical supervision

At the same time, administration is also fundamentally different from the technical supervision of operations. The administrator has a good idea of technical supervision but takes no part in it. He is primarily a social engineer, a knowledgeable and skillful unifier and leader of a social collective that consists of many partial technicians. His task is to build a sound organizational plan of his enterprise and select appropriate personnel for his staff. With the help of this staff, he works long and hard to find appropriate human resources, educate workers, and unite them into a harmonious whole. He is to charge everybody with a clear-cut area of responsibility, set definite objectives for every team and provide relevant directives, continuously coordinate the work of various departments and carefully control the execution of his orders.

His greatest fear is to succumb to the prejudiced mentality of the isolated worker, a self-proclaimed know-all who scatters his energy over thousands of petty technical problems. The administrator must feel like a ship captain who directs his vessel and controls its progress. His greatest concern is to avoid believing that he is the best expert in every field. It is his right and duty, for instance, to give orders to the engine room concerning the speed of the ship, control performance, and conduct inspections. His visit to the engine room to teach the mechanic how to handle the boiler, however, would be nothing but counterproductive. An idea that the administrator should or has the right to personally instruct the worker on technical aspects of his job is probably the worst legacy of the disappearing era of authoritarian management.

P.M. Kerzhentsev **(13)** provides a graphic illustration to this point in his "Principles of organization": "To know how to get rid of the burden of small things is a most essential quality of any leader and organizer.

A telling dialogue on this topic took place between Morgan and a Federal Court lawyer. Morgan was questioned with regard to a purchase of 15 million dollars' worth of shares in the North Pacific Railroad.

- How much did the shares cost?

- I haven't the slightest idea.

- How much money did your company make on this transaction?

- I do not know.

- Did you make a million or ten million?

- I say I don't know. I don't go into details. I said: buy them. Mr. Still knows the details, he'll tell you."

This examples shows, Kerzhentsev writes (p. 93) that Morgan freed himself of smaller problems by delegating their solution to trusted assistants.

The times of the isolated worker are gone for good. An administrator's job is *fundamentally* different from that of any technical expert. A modern leader of a large collective labor organization should know how to draw a clear border between these two kinds of expertise and never cross it.

This is why the leader of a large business who does not restrict himself to issuing orders and following up on their execution but meddles with the technical execution process is a bad administrator. He is a lone rather than social worker. He frustrates work rather than organizes it. He bothers his subordinates, whatever his good intentions are, destabilizes their work by causing confusion and lack of confidence, the worst enemies of organization.

At the same time, he neglects *his own job.* Since he squanders his talents on trifle matters, he trails his business instead of leading it forward. He has neither time nor energy for the most important things – deliberation, orientation, research and planning.

He is like a tired horse pulled down by the cart on a steep slope. He has no power over the rudder. His ship is driven, like helpless driftwood, by currents and winds. *The organizer's job is fundamentally different from that of operating personnel.* This truth should be memorized and understood by any leader.

4. Types of organizers during the transition period

1. The *detailed leader* is definitely a legacy from the past. His ambitions and techniques almost invariably reveal that he belongs to the "isolated worker" category described above in sufficient detail.

The other two types belong to the social worker category:

2. The "romantic" organizer, to use Oswald's expression **(14)**, can *inspire* and *infect people* with his enthusiasm. His staff usually consists of people with less initiative. Current work, guidance and control are usually delegated to his closest assistants and the staff, while the organizer deals with some new "trailblazing" project and concentrates on cooperation with the team to address new issues.

An organization under this kind of leadership is generally flexible and dynamic but somewhat lacks stability.

3. The *regulatory type* organizer, according to Ostwald, has a "classic" character. His staff usually consists of active and dynamic workers handling the immediate management of the enterprise. The leader restricts himself to coordination, regulation, control and balancing various forces.

Such an organization is generally quite stable and dynamic, though tends to have less flexibility, initiative and maneuverability than the previously described type.

122

Whatever the differences, it is quite clear that both progressive types of management pertain to *social organizations.*

Accordingly, they require major changes in the mentality of management personnel.

The old type of administrator has no place in the new system.

Lazurskiy **(15)** notes that "administrators" belong to a psychological group of "power mongers". "Their goal, - he writes, - is not so much to organize management but *carry it out* by implementing earlier plans and assumptions. In contrast to other mental types, power mongers concentrate all their spiritual energy on using their influence to lead other people to a set objective as vigorously as possible. Hence their determination and self-confidence, confidence and the lack of doubts that are so typical of many theoreticians and organizers who have to check their conclusions and redo their projects several times to make sure they are correct. Hence the well-known conservatism of administrators, their hostility towards criticism of traditional principles and ways, their utter confidence in the absolute accuracy of their method. They also tend to be proud and self-assured, sometimes excessively. A person who covets power and has to fight against others cannot but protect his ego from any attempted assault; it is equally natural for him to demonstrate and emphasize his superiority."

The administrator portrayed by Lazurskiy definitely belongs to the past. Industrialism has transformed this age-old figure of an "isolated worker" into a completely different type of an organizer and a social leader. As we saw above, industrialism rejects conservatism as something incompatible with the demand for continuous technological and organizational progress, as well as the principle of power and obedience since it is alien to the cooperative labor nature of an industrial enterprise.

Industrial development wants the administrator to retain features that Lazurskiy defines as "capacity for long and high concentration of willpower, propensity for struggle and resistance, self-control" but combine them with the features of a *social worker,* i.e., "affectivity and good communication abilities, love for company, activity, mobility, concentration on human relations as the basis of social life."

5. Organizational structure

What is the job of an organizer? First and foremost, he must carefully design the organizational structure of his business.

An English manual on administration recommends the following first and foremost rule. "To design a proper organizational structure for an institution is not as easy as it might seem. Lines, circles, and squares with legends hardly matter. An institution should be designed so that each of its parts would function automatically. This means that every department and every worker should have as much independence as possible. This does not mean that everybody would do whatever he fancies. Rather, he should do exactly what is needed in a proper way without waiting to be urged or ordered. This is called *automatism of operations.* An institution should be similar to a machine that does everything on its own, from feeding to processing. Every administrator should, in a certain sense, feel that he is positioned *outside rather than within* his department. He is responsible for building this automatic machine, regulate its operation, control execution and incessantly strive for its improvement."

6. How to automate an organization

First of all, a proper chain of operations should be designed.

1.   The initial step is to prepare a clear written document that should define the *rights, objectives, and work procedures for each department.* These regulations should be formal, on the one hand, and be always open to revision and

updates, on the other hand. Such division of labor should make sure that the subject of work is completely covered by the joint efforts of all departments without any responsibilities overlapping. Each issue should be immediately handled by a one and only department without any duplication by another or, even worse, more than one other unit. Any need in coordination among departments is a clear sign of bad organization. The inevitable alignment of strategic plans and departmental functions belongs to *preparation and planning,* while coordination of current operations is in no way acceptable. Any need for such coordination must be eliminated by a clear-cut division of responsibilities. Moreover, the department responsible for a job must be entitled to *handle* it independently without any clearance from other departments or senior management.

Again, no organization is viable without clear internal regulations on principal departments, like no machine or house can be built without a good plan and detailed drawings.

2. Clear separation of duties among divisions and subdivisions based on the same principle of independence and broad rights should also be carried out within every department. Each department must have its own regulations that would be subject to periodic updates.

3. The preparation for creating the organizational structure does not stop here. Now we need to compose job descriptions and instructions for every employee that would specify his position, role, rights, responsibilities and functions.

It is for a reason that companies abroad spend years to develop job descriptions and instructions for every worker, from general manager to delivery man. These documents are the cornerstone of the worker's independence.

4. Finally, it is critical to devise *a sound scheme of handling every type of issues in terms of stages and deadlines.*

These organizational preparations can be compared with laying rail tracks to let the work move ahead. One can never pay too much attention to the strength of these tracks or take too much care of them.

7. Independence of automatic collective labor system

Now let us move to our main point. Recall that the system must function automatically, and each work unit must proceed without waiting for orders from the top.

This requires the following:

1) A central body that regulates the manufacturing flow and (a) assumes all the functions of planning, issuing instructions and developing general policies, and (b) deals with operations records and control over execution;

2) A job should be sent *directly* to the proper department rather than pass through any intermediate administrative stages. Execution based on a given plan and directives is the responsibility of operations personnel only.

Operations personnel should come up with questions to senior management only in case of confusion. This is always a bad sign that becomes even worse if the problem has to be addressed by senior management. It is, in fact, a warning to the administration that something is wrong with the organization, the plan, the directives or the instructions.

In a regular situation, the administration does not interfere with actual operations. It monitors *the essence* of the production process based on reports covering the quantity and quality of jobs as well as work progress rather than the *techniques* of work.

8. How to select and retain personnel

Careful selection of personnel is critical to any business. The best drawing is useless if a machine or a house is built from an inferior material. The result would be a cheap imitation of a watch instead of a chronometer. Likewise, no seven-story house can be built from dried clay rather than firebrick. Social engineering in this sense does not differ much from industrial engineering. A strong structure needs good human material. We should learn how to build sturdy structures, not flimsy wooden cabins.

Using whatever is at hand in a hope of "replacing" it with something better in the future is not a good habit. Can a machine work properly if its parts are replaced every day? Certainly not. Individual parts are not as important as the harmony of the whole mechanism. A machine tool is appreciated exactly because of this harmony that cannot be created overnight even by the most experienced engineer. Old violins have a great value, but an association of people is even more sophisticated than a musical instrument. Carnegie was right when he said that he would need a generation to restore the organization of his factories **(16)**. The administrator must give up the bad habit of individualistic thinking when he does not see the forest for the trees, i.e., sees individual Ivanovs and Petrovs rather than that intangible factor that unites all Ivanovs and Petrovs in a harmonious *social organization.* Fayol correctly argued that the administrator must continuously take care of mutual adjustment between bosses and subordinates as well as among bosses and subordinates themselves. A worker or a manager should be selected with an intention to retain him for good rather than replace him at any moment. Once carefully selected, personnel must be kept permanently.

Only stabilized personnel can create a stable and efficient social organization.

Advanced companies in the industrial society do not just check whether a candidate for the position has appropriate experience. They use careful research (often taking advantage of psychotechnics) to find out if the candidate is psychologically fit for this position in terms of a broad range of qualities.

The internal fitness of a person for a given job is a serious factor. Ford Motor Company is widely regarded as an absolutely "mechanized" institution. Yet its factories pay great attention to work preferences indicated by job applicants.

The *stability* of personnel is just as important as the appropriate *selection* of human resources.

In its report on waste and losses in the U.S. industry, the Hoover commission **(17)** found, in particular, that *factories with the greatest turnover of personnel have the least order and the lowest efficiency per worker.*

9. Work environment

A positive work environment is at least as important for a good administrator as a sound organizational structure and meticulously selected personnel.

At this point, the lone leader's prejudices and lack of insight into the nature of collective labor are even more harmful. While doing his best to provide as many technical and sanitary amenities to managers, he is usually quite oblivious to the comfort of blue-collar workers. We have seen above, however, that the actual work is done by the collective rather than the administrator who just provides guidance, and work environment has a major impact on performance. The work team at a factory or agency needs no less care than the mechanism of any machine. In addition to work safety, any team member requires a stimulating rather than a depressing work environment. Employees should be encouraged, not neglected.

Today's advanced factories are built so as to ensure full availability of light and fresh air, they have sound insulation and provide supplementary tools to make work easier. Some German firms regularly put flowers on the desks of their workers, particularly women.

No doubt this is done for practical business reasons, that is, a desire to improve productivity and motivate the worker, rather than out of idealism or love for the "little brothers". Here is a clear example.

At a garment factory with over a hundred workers, productivity dropped sharply with the advent of summer heat, exactly at a time when top-notch performance was needed to prepare for the fall season. Various attempts to address this problem gave no tangible results.

A detailed analysis demonstrated, however, that ambient temperature had a major impact on performance: On an occasional cloudy day, output promptly rebounded to the winter level. A powerful ventilation system was then installed at the shop. The output instantly increased by 20%, the proportion of rejects dropped and the workers' morale improved greatly.

A German insurance company in New York in 1910 employed 80 people, of which 10% were always on sick leave. Once proper ventilation was installed, absenteeism dropped to almost zero.

Some factories improved the lighting system. On one occasion, an increase from 4,000 to 12,000 lumen led to a 27% increase in productivity. In another case, a 25% productivity gain was reached by simply moving the employees away from a source of noise.

Advanced factories pay special attention to the alternation of work and rest periods and set up special lounges for good relaxation. Continuous work without rest has a pronounced negative impact on performance.

Some businesses introduce mandatory rest periods, e.g., two 15-20 minutes breaks a day for stenographers, switchboard operators, sales clerks, and packers, or hourly short breaks for elevator attendants. At a steel mill in Vandergrift 20-30 minutes of work are followed by rest periods of the same length. During these periods the workers relax in the garden, play sports and the like.

The effect of 10-minute breaks between work periods on productivity during the 10-hour work day was studied in the United States. It was found that productivity increased by 3% after the first break, by 17% and 26% after subsequent breaks. Once 20-minute breaks were introduced at a bleaching factory after every 80 minutes of work, productivity increased by 60%. Now, a British military supplies factory mandated 15-minute breaks after every 45 minutes of work. Its employees paid according to a piece-rate system, were quite unhappy, since they thought their wages would drop. In fact, their performance showed a considerable improvement and the wages increased accordingly.

An interesting story happened during the war when two groups of soldiers at the front line were proposed to compete in digging trenches over a certain period of time. The officer in charge of the first group divided his men into three shifts, so each shift could enjoy 10-minute breaks after each 5 minutes of work. Through such a staggered arrangement, one shift was always at work. The officer in charge of the second team made his people work as usual without any special work distribution system. His soldiers were supposed to dig as hard as they could, have irregular rest periods once they felt exhausted and then go back to work. The first group easily won. The experiment was repeated at a bottle factory with similar results.

10. Psychological climate

Important as it is, work environment must be supported by the right psychological climate, this barely sensible yet crucial factor that is called "l'esprit du corps" - «the spirit of the hive» or corporate team spirit in the foreign literature.

The essential main goal of day-to-day administrative activities is to create this atmosphere of friendly mass cooperation.   It is a great and fine art to combine the universally acknowledged business and moral *authority* of the administrator with the broadest grassroots *initiative* possible.

It is not nearly enough to divide an organization into proper structural units, draft dozens of paper instructions and regulations, man all desks or machines (even with well-selected personnel) and provide a minimum of amenities to workers.   These are little more than *prerequisites* of good collective cooperation that has yet to be created and sustained. A social machine thus designed must be inspired with a "live soul" of ownership and work enthusiasm.

The following examples illustrate the importance of collective work attitudes that do not yield to "mechanical" means and external pressure.

"A shop usually produced 5,000 items a week. The factory administration decided to open a similar shop with identical machinery and hired some inexperienced workers who knew little about traditions or the production process. After a six-month pilot period, the new shop produced 13,000 items a week; the old one continued to produce 5,000."

A good indicator of team spirit is the rate of employee turnover. Here is an example. Two gangs were making identical products at a car factory next to each other under similar general and technological conditions. Each gang had 18 workers from 18 to 21 years old. The first one was headed by a middle-aged foreman with excellent technical skills but no special leadership qualities. The second one was headed by a charismatic 25-year-old, a keen athlete. He enjoyed immense respect and popularity among his workers and turned his gang into a true team where staff turnover averaged just 3 to 4 men a year as opposed to 9-10 men in the second gang.

Again, the administrator's key job is to ignite and sustain ownership and work enthusiasm. He must be a born leader in whatever business, even the manufacturing and distribution of shoe polish.

Mind it that team spirit and enthusiasm can hardly be instilled and fostered by the lone leader, with his Olympic grandeur, bossy harshness or paternalism. This style of management is gone forever. The new style is that of collective work, based on the cooperative nature of large-scale industries. Economic activities belong to social work just as much as political, military or cooperative activities.

The administrator should never forget that it is *the labor collective* under his guidance *that does the actual work.* This collective needs more than logistical and technological support. *It needs a continuous supply of sound incentives that would reassure the workers and foster their sense of ownership.*

American engineers that started the NOT movement were aware of the immense productivity losses in the absence of true incentives. They addressed the issue by developing a better wage system, which was a major achievement. However, *all of them including Taylor were slaves to the individualistic philosophy based on the concept of the isolated worker motivated solely by monetary interests.* They discovered the stimulating effect of the differentiated wage system but failed to go any further.

Of late, the NOT movement has made considerable progress in this area. "The first workers in the field of scientific management tried to ignore the democratic implications of science. Their successors know better. Today every industrial engineer bases his work upon cooperation with all the human elements involved. He has become the firmest friend of industrial democracy. The moment the methods of science were extended directly to the problems of personnel relations, it was inevitable that democracy should follow," wrote Simons.

"For executives in every field are coming increasingly to see that the source of efficiency, economy and goodwill which is particularly elusive and at the same time peculiarly critical, is the attitude with which the individual's and group's energy without the human consent of those who run the mechanism is no more effective than scissors with only one blade. There is a vital necessity for actively enlisting and inspiriting the working force. The workers must cooperate," write Tead and Metcalf.

Modern managers treat a worker not just as a person selling his labor but as a member of a collective. They want the worker to be interested in his job and that of his co-workers as much as possible and give him maximum freedom from micro-management.

Apart from doing his immediate job, the worker should be aware of its social meaning and have a sense of achievement. As we have seen above, performance deteriorates with increasing fatigue, whether muscular or psychological.

A successful day seems like a holiday, a bad day seems like a shift on a treadmill. A person unhappy with his job gets exhausted much sooner than the one who is keen on his work and its challenges.

To be satisfied with one's work, a person should

1) understand its social meaning,

2) have good machine-operating skills,

3) deal with tasks that are realistic yet not too easy. Satisfaction arises from the sense of one's power to meet challenges.

The administrator should always remember these ideas when dealing with his subordinates.

However, this applies to general corporate policies as well:

1) Every worker should always be well informed about the technical and economic situation at the factory, its achievements and failures, much like news from the front are the universal focus of attention during the war.

British and US corporations have recently introduced corporate newspapers as well as regular discussions of economic and technological matters at committee and other meetings. A bonus system encourages workers to submit improvement projects in any area to special commissions.

Here is a typical announcement from one of the factories:

"We invite EVERY WORKER TO MAKE PRODUCTION IMPROVEMENT PROPOSALS!

We need your support and advice.

Any critical comment or suggestion is welcome.

You are in the midst of work.

You can point to a variety of flaws better than anyone.

Pick up a proposal form, fill it out, seal the envelope and drop into the proposal box or send to the proposal commission by mail.

Every suggestion will receive full attention. If you disagree with the reasons for its rejection, visit the commission in person.

If the receipt of your proposal is not acknowledged, tell the commission.

Do not expect a prompt positive or negative reply. It takes time to consider the issue and collect the necessary data."

The improvement commission at an American cash register company receives *six thousand projects a year;* about *one third* of them are fully or partially implemented.

The General Electric corporate magazine writes the following about the company's values:

«What are our values?

We are a part of a huge organization serving mankind. We make light bulbs. It seems like a pedestrian, boring and unromantic occupation. However, think of a recent case when a child swallowed a needle by accident. A doctor was called. With great care he inserted a special probe into the child's throat to extract the needle. A slightly wrong motion would have killed the patient. Yet because the doctor was equipped with miniature light bulbs you are making, he could clearly see inside the child's throat and saved his life.

You, the light bulb manufacturers, help keep railway and marine transportation safe... You improve your work environment at factories and offices... Thanks to you, millions of men and women live a nicer, more comfortable and active life..."

2) Every worker should have appropriate skills. However, he should be given every opportunity to improve these skills. Along with the training system described above, modern factories invest a lot in continuing education and generously supply their libraries with books on engineering and economics. They also send employees on educational tours to similar corporations.

Here is a graphic announcement from the National Cash Register Company (US) to its employees:

"In order to compare your work with that at other factories and to learn about the best new practices we are planning to organize an educational trip to East Coast factories for the staff from the following departments (spouses are welcome)."

After listing the departments and the number of participants from each department, the announcement goes on as follows:

"Tour participants shall be elected by the staff from each department. We would like them to pay close attention to manufacturing processes at the factories, learn about production methods and wage systems, and, once back home, give a full account to their colleagues. We want an open-minded and impartial report on all your observations.

We want better work conditions in every department and shop of our factory, so if they exist elsewhere we would like to know."

Apart from traditional classroom courses, modern companies often arrange conferences for informal down-to-earth discussions on major issues. Such conferences occasionally evolve into permanent employee education groups such as the Progress Club at the National Cash Register Company.

3) Systematic competition between individuals or teams, an excellent tool that increases productivity and stimulates interest in work, is deeply rooted in the collective nature of industrial labor.

A classic example of competition between teams dates back to the construction of the Panama channel when a group of military engineers digging the channel from the Atlantic side competed with that of civil engineers working from the Pacific side. Daily reports on the amount of dirt removed were sent to the workers and compared to provide a continuous incentive to work harder.

Carnegie attributed the entire success of his organization to a consistent policy of group and individual competition that put upward pressure on productivity and created collective excitement conducive to a strong team spirit.

Carnegie introduced weekly and monthly reports for every department large and small, asked to make them as comparable as possible and took great interest in total output as well as unit costs in terms of raw materials, time and labor. By using these figures to show the best achievements to those groups or executives lagging behind and arouse the sense of individual and collective responsibility, he created a highly vigorous and tightly knit company.

Packard car factories also take advantage of group competition. "A team charged with full assembly is always proud to deliver a shining new car on time to win."

Group competition for higher speed and better product quality, be it on a local, regional or national scale, has the same effect.

The use of role models is also a good incentive in collective labor. Role models play an important part in group competition. Moreover, advanced companies take good care of their best workers and, aware of Napoleon's words that every soldier hoped to be made a general, establish an elaborate system of promotion to put, as they say in English, *the right man in the right place.*

The issue of merit-based wage increases and promotions is now high on the agenda in industrial countries.

For instance, the White Motor Company (USA) believes that "the value of a worker grows with seniority. If a semi-annual review shows that an employee was not recommended for a raise or promotion by the foreman, the issue is subject to a special investigation." This system has been quite useful.

A company makes progress if its human resources do. Promotion is needed for two reasons: It satisfies the employees' natural desire for a better pay as well as for a higher position. It also makes a person more confident, proud and eager to continue professional development. Promotions, therefore, improve the general quality of workforce.

Large companies have special schedules for the possible promotion of each manager subject to a review of personal qualities and special skills required at every step. These schedules are circulated among personnel. On the other hand, human resources management includes planning possible future promotions for each employee and recording them in his file. This work is closely integrated with awareness campaigns and systematic continuous education.

Last but not least, probably the most important incentive that shall be discussed in detail in the next chapter is *the involvement of workers with management,* their active influence on the production process and collective responsibility.

This issue is closely associated with the factory committees' movement. The number of such committees has been growing steadily. For example, in 1922, there were 725 factory committees in the USA compared to 225 in 1919.

11. New style of business cooperation

To sum up, the development of industrialism has been destroying the traditional ways of work and management typical of the "isolated worker" and emphasizing the collective nature of concentrated production. A special applied science has emerged to study the laws of such production. We should therefore expect an imminent cultural revolution whose ramifications and specific forms are too early to predict at this point, at the very beginning of the rising wave of future economic culture.

So far, we can only provide a very general definition of these changes as *collectivization of labor* and the emergence of a new style of economic cooperation.

The new style of work in manufacturing and elsewhere is that of social work. Labor is a service to society. Economic cooperation is social work. A factory, a shop, an office, a store or an agency are exactly the same social collectives as the Party, the army, a trade union or a cooperative. The style of social work characteristic of the Party, the Army or the cooperative movement is penetrating deeply into economic activities and starts dominating labor and personal relations in manufacturing, commerce, government, and the service sector. Labor as work and labor as a social service are merging into one. Only labor as a social service and meaningful cooperation can ensure maximum productivity in an industrial society with its concentrated work collectives.

Just recall the incredibly difficult conditions (in general as well as financial terms) that prevail in party work or in a real cooperative where people devote all their life to the cause and sacrifice everything to serve this cause. Mind it, they have few romantic reasons for that. The job of an underground typographer, a rank-and-file agitator or organizer is boring and inconspicuous. There is hardly any fun in purchasing and packing soap, flour and salt for a small coop.

Yet these are ideal (at least for our times) social machines held together by a shared philosophy and powered by the united spirit of collective cooperation.

Why?

First, these machines are truly automatic. Each component has its own technical function and receives only general guidance from the supervisor.

Second, workers are selected with utmost care, with a view to retain them for as long as possible.

Third, the administrator, in this case, is always aware of the harmony in the organization. At the same time, he knows every worker's personality in great detail. One of his most important day-to-day tasks is to fine-tune these personalities so they could form a solid working unity.

Fourth, everybody knows the social objective and techniques of the organization as a whole and the meaning of his own work at any given moment. Moreover, one way or the other, he takes part in forging these objectives and techniques. They are not alien to the worker; they capture everybody in a powerful and efficient stream of action.

Fifth, every worker is used to the fullest of his capacity. The right men are in the right places.

Sixth, training and retraining goes on at any given moment throughout the system to master work skills even further.

Seventh, everyone at any given moment has a strong sense of ownership. Bonds between workers become stronger as the workflow gets more intense.

These are the principles of social work that industrial development establishes in any organization by means of scientific management to create a new style of business cooperation.

12. Administration

Henri Fayol and the French school of experimental administration outline five functions of management (administration).

Two of them refer to *planning* and *controlling*. The administrator designs a plan of action based on the analysis of the current situation and follows up on implementation.

The other three deal with social organization at the company and the collective labor machine. They include *organizing* personnel, *coordination* between various units and *commanding*.

The French school suggests the following definition of the content and social nature of administration.

Collective life is a result of willful actions of a group rather than a single individual. "This is particularly relevant today when the outcome of collective activities depends to a greater extent on the masses rather than the manager. A modern worker cooperates rather than obeys."

On the other hand, collective life implies harmony that cannot emerge on its own. The performance of a group is not a simple arithmetic sum of individual performances. A group of people inspired with the best of intentions but lacking an organizing center is anarchic and powerless. A social union must be charged with the same kind of purposeful harmony that is found in nature and reproduced in man-made machines.

This calls for a special profession of an administrator who must influence personnel in order to establish a harmonious unity in a company, stimulate individual and collective efforts and concentrate all the separate wills in a certain direction. These functions become particularly critical in large collectives.

This administrative influence must be all-embracing, continuous, sound and strictly methodical. At the same time, it should be based on firm scientific knowledge and careful experimental studies, as is fit in our times of mass organizations and rationalism.

Collective life is a result of willful actions of a group rather than a single individual. It means a clean break is needed with traditional formal discipline and blind obedience.

The collective life of a company must be awoken to develop freely. Discipline should become a voluntary matter. Interest in labor, collective initiative and workman's pride should be fostered in employees.

These are the objectives of the administrator's daily work in any economic organization.

13. The administrative staff

Administration had a more than modest place in Taylor's system. As an individualist, he failed to notice the collective nature of industrial production and believed that administration was a minor component of general planning and management. A worker in his system was always an isolated person. As for work incentives, Taylor reduced them to higher pay and bonuses.

The further development of industrialism, however, has emphasized the collective nature of industrial labor on an ever increasing scale. It has become clear that administration is a special field that requires special techniques, attitudes, and structures.

Accordingly, large companies establish special administration staff along with technical and production staff (see chapters 2 and 3) to concentrate on personnel issues and collective labor incentives.

Personnel issues and social matters that used to be scattered among a variety of managers are now consistently addressed from a single center.

This staff has a lot of work to do. Here is an approximate list of its departments and their functions:

1. Labor safety and health: 1) providing health care to workers and their families; 2) periodic sanitary inspections at the factory by (a) the labor safety engineer and (b) members of the safety board; 3) systematic monitoring of the work environment including that for women and manual laborers (cleanliness, ventilation, lighting, heating, lavatories, showers, drinking fountains, lockers, general sanitation); 4) periodic medical check-ups for workers; 5) accident statistics and improvement of safety measures; 6) labor safety awareness, drafting safety instructions for all categories of workers; 7) prevention of epidemics; 8) studying occupational diseases, developing measures to control fatigue, optimize rest and nutrition.

Of particular interest in this area is establishing of permanent labor safety committees representing workers from every shop and organizing on-site sanitation awareness campaigns.

2. Use of workforce: 1) statistics of vacancies and labor turnover with breakdown by profession; 2) preparation of standard job requirements; 3) preparation of standard job descriptions specifying work conditions and pay schedules; 4) labor market studies; 5) interviewing, testing and selecting candidates; 6) maintaining employee statistics and personal records; 7) reviewing decisions on transfers, dismissals and reinstatements, keeping statistics of reasons for quitting or dismissal; 8) maintaining a system for training new workers and supervising them during the trial period; 9) design and implementation of a system for promotions and transfers.

Industrial countries currently pay close attention to the issue of personnel retention as a key to higher productivity. Hoover's Commission on non-productive losses in US industry noted that it can cost up to 50 to 150 dollars to accommodate an experienced worker and a semi-trained worker respectively at a new job.

Any move to another company, therefore, is an unjustifiable loss to the national economy. The commission estimated that such losses in the US steel industry alone amounted to 100 million a year. Alexander, an American engineer, claims that retraining due to low retention rates costs US industries from 400 million to 1 billion dollars a year. In fact, the total losses due to employee turnover are much higher. Hoover's Commission notes that *companies with the highest employee turnover rate are ill organized and have the least productivity.*

Efforts to retain personnel focus mainly in two areas: 1) developing a system of regular pay raises and promotions

141

to positions of greater responsibility, and 2) fostering the sense of ownership in each worker from the very beginning of employment. Some companies take newly hired workers on a tour of the factory to introduce them to its general structure, internal regulations, work conditions and techniques. During the trial period they are subject to intense comprehensive training.

3. ***Close attention is paid to education and retraining.*** The appropriate department in cooperation with the employee committee addresses issues such as 1) introducing new employees to the internal structure of the company, its place in the national economy and the manufacturing technologies used; 2) publication of a corporate paper or magazine; 3) operating an improvement proposal committee; 4) regular dissemination of corporate information and reports at meetings and in publications; 5) establishing education groups or clubs; 6) circulation of economic and engineering literature among employees; 7) running short-term courses for the purposes of a) transfers, b) promotions, c) inspector and supervisor training; 8) sanitation and safety awareness work, 9) general continuous education.

Other forms of education apart from short-term training include a free exchange of opinions at conferences where presentations on technical, economic or administrative issues are discussed; special tours around the factory as well as to similar factories; professional congresses of experts in particular fields; competitions in speed or skills and so on.

Corporate periodicals and improvement proposal commissions deserve a special attention in this regard.

4. The labor research department deals with setting output and pay rates. Its employees 1) analyze the work process and set output rates using time studies; 2) study fatigue; 3) study pay rates and provide appropriate consultations; 4) study general work conditions; 5) monitor workers' budgets and price indices; 6) maintain communications with research centers and other learned institutions dealing with labor.

5. The social services department is responsible for 1) profit-sharing arrangements; 2) organization of employee cooperatives; 3) monitoring the use of company housing; 4) organization of corporate outings; 5) corporate vacation services; 6) allocation of vegetable patches; 7) workers' household improvements.

6. *The conciliation commission* represents workers, managers and administration. It is designed to 1) approve and enforce internal regulations; 2) conduct hearings on conflicts and misunderstandings; 3) endorse workload and pay schedules; 4) approve dismissals.

All this work implies strong participation by workers and other employees elected by shops or appointed by the factory committee.

As already mentioned, such committees make a major contribution to management and administration, and their number in the USA increased from 225 in 1919 to 725 in 1922.

Note that administration works in close cooperation with the production department.

14. Administration staff in the army

We have already noted the progressive features of the army as the first organization of broad, powerful and continuous collective action in history. The army was also the first to raise the issue of staff work as well as that of systematic influence on personnel as the key factors of success and even the very existence of this enormous social entity.

"The army," writes Trotsky **(18)**, "is based not only on hardware and an organizational structure but also on collective morale. Regulations, the line of command and orders may regulate just one third if not one-tenth of human relations: Formal discipline and subordination can hardly prevail without psychological bondage, collective responsibility, friendship, and trust in the right cause."

It is well-known that Napoleon believed that material factors account for no more than one-fourth of the victory. This view is quite common among the military now. It is graphically illustrated by N. Alexander in his paper "Psychological impact

of combat environment on the effectiveness of infantry fire."
("Izvestiya" collection, No. 6-7).

In particular, he quotes Captain Missile of the French General Staff who wrote about the Russian-Japanese war, "Experience shows that once the attacking side succeeds as close to the defending side as 75-150 steps, defense collapses. Even the bravest of people get nervous and lose self-control. At distances from which single targets can indeed be hit, even veteran soldiers lose their marksmanship."

An active participant in the last war (1914-1917) testifies that today's French rifle fire is so fatal that no trench could ever be seized if its defendants were to aim properly until the last minute. Most soldiers, however, hide their heads behind the breastwork, hold their rifles barrel up and shoot into the air. The closer the enemy, the more often this happens. This is why the attacking side sustains more casualties in reserves than in the wave. If just 20 soldiers in a company of 200 (10%) keep their composure, any frontal attack would be foiled even at a very short distance. People usually start getting nervous when the approaching enemy is 1200-1400 steps away and can be seen clearly."

The average percentage of hits in modern wars is 0.2-0.4%. Incidentally, the author notes that military fire dispersal at close range, in contrast to civil fire, is inversely proportional to distance.

He arrives at a highly reasonable conclusion (that does sound odd in terms of today's common sense), "Adversaries in a battle want to frustrate each other's social organization by putting psychological pressure on the enemy. Therefore, killing in war is not an aim but rather a means of suppressing the collective will of the enemy and cause panic." In other words, the goal is to destroy the enemy's social organization.

Therefore, administration aimed at creating and maintaining "psychological bondage, collective responsibility, friendship, and trust in the right cause" has always been prominent in the army. "The power of a military or economic organization is measured by the extent of cohesion between individual units and between their members."

144

Good administration is particularly important for today's million-strong armies that deal with intense and protracted conflicts. The revolutionary instinct prompted the Red Army to establish such administration in the form of political education units and commissar positions. Unfortunately, this unique experience has yet to be properly described and studied.

The USA made similar steps during the World War, albeit on a more conscious basis, by organizing the Morale branch of the General Staff (in fact, a social psychology department) described by Colonel Munson in his remarkable book "Management of Men".

"All this makes it particularly important," he writes, "that an administrative organization should exist which will insure the systematic adoption of measures to increase harmony, cooperation and efficiency, supervise the work or effect of various agencies and factors influencing the state of mind, and remove elements of discontent and points of painful contact. The mechanism necessary in morale work is much like that required in any engineering problem and is neither simpler nor less technical because its results are mental."

Munson provides a draft classification of factors affecting morale as follows:

A. Environment

1. Physical

Food, clothing, shelter, cleanliness, pay, recreation, surroundings, climate and weather conditions

2. General social environment

Relations with civilian communities, public entertainment, library, reading, writing and studying facilities, education, passes, post exchange, visitors, clubs.

B. Administrative organization

Leadership agencies

Sympathetic relationship between officers and men; example of officers; proper use of punishment and reprimand; encouragement and reward; promotions; discipline; confidence of men in the leadership ability.

Psychological agencies

Instincts: use of, diverting or repressing the natural instincts; esprit de corps; interest and pride in the military service generally; ideals, goals, standards, personal pride and organization pride; inspirational ceremonies, reviews, parades; initiative and individual expression; rumors and gossip; propaganda; extent of friendly consolidation.

The Morale Branch of the General Staff directs the administrative activities of all officers and some special services such as education agencies, medical agencies, supply services or the Red Cross.

Chapter VII. NOT in Soviet Russia: organizational issues[70]

1. *Russian NOT yesterday and today*

---

[70] We decided to omit Chapter VI "Capitalism, Socialism and NOT" as a purely ideological exercise of little theoretical value. It seems likely that this ideological masquerade was a peculiar "bribe" that Vitke offered to Bolshevik censors for an opportunity to publish his concept. The omitted chapter is full of worn-out Communist buzzwords that can be reduced to a statement that capitalism in incapable of implementing the true NOT. Only socialism can ostensibly do it. The book was published but Chapter VI failed to deceive Communist NOT vigilantes. As we know all too well, the original theory was destroyed, apparently along with its creator.

Russian NOT has obviously entered a new stage of development. Its present is vastly different from its past and even cautious estimates indicate that the nascent future of Russian NOT will involve further fundamental changes.

What are the causes for this turning point and what are its features and meaning? What is the driving force behind it? What organizational challenges faces NOT during this new period?

Let us consider these issues.

NOT as an international movement emerged from practice for practical purposes.

Its objectives are: 1) to develop an applied science concerned with collective labor; 2) to arm the *practical manager* with this science in order to systematically improve collective labor across economies.

As any applied science (e.g., agriculture or medicine) NOT is capable of a fast and healthy evolution only if its theory and practice develop hand in hand, closely interact and have enough room to grow simultaneously. This close contact and mutual diffusion between theory and practice are required in any applied discipline. Any imbalance in this area hurts the discipline as a whole, i.e., slows down its development and deflects it from the right course.

This is exactly what was happening to NOT "yesterday".

Leaving aside certain exciting and symptomatic pre-revolutionary efforts and focusing on NOT during the revolutionary period, let us note that it was largely *separated and isolated from the practice it was meant to serve and improve. NOT's "yesterday" involved no broad practical efforts.* Industry during that period did not care for any scientific (or even elementary) improvements and therefore ignored NOT.

This does not mean that NOT's "yesterday" was theoretical or, as they say now, "academic". NOT in Russia could hardly conduct meaningful original research since it was lacking a practical base. Indeed, theoretical achievements in this area have been patchy and insignificant. A lot of work has yet to be done in order to fundamentally revamp the traditional NOT developed in capitalist countries. What we have now is, at best, some embryonic forms of future Russian NOT schools. Academic institutions in the country barely feel any influence of NOT. The same applies to industrial management practices.

While neither an applied nor a theoretical discipline, the current NOT is a rather amorphous field that had no time to differentiate. It seems the best definition for it would be "ideological".

Indeed, Russian NOT owes its existence to the tenacity of its enthusiasts rather than external recognition or the existence of a recognized *professional function.* Russia hardly has any professional managers. Russian academics have just begun to contemplate a place for NOT in the convoluted system of modern sciences. No wonder that all NOT research institutions except for that in Ukraine **(19)** do not belong to the Ministry of Education system, while occasional NOT departments at universities limit themselves to teaching only.

NOT's "yesterday" was a period of struggle for survival and self-assertion when the movement was taking all its energy from within and fought for survival in a hostile or indifferent environment.

NOT's "yesterday" was the *ideological stage.*

Its isolation from common management practice is easy to illustrate.

1. Nothing has been heard since the revolution about any grassroots scientific management initiatives. If we are not mistaken, the only exception refers to certain efforts by staff engineers at the Ministry of Transportation that, however, failed to trigger any large-scale practical improvements.

2. NOT activities are largely concentrated in two types of institutions: 1) research facilities and 2) line consultancies.

3. Rather unexpectedly, NOT research facilities proved to be more vital than line consultancies despite their weaker links with industrial practices and relatively limited financing.

We believe it is the best evidence that the movement was ideological. Its energy came from within rather than from without. NOT agents trust that their work for the future is more important than any current practical results.

2. NOT and work culture

NOT's overall environment has changed dramatically. If these changes persist for a long time, they will certainly affect the nature of this discipline **(20)**.

Indeed, a long period of NOT's isolation from managerial practices is coming to an end. Managers now want NOT to systematically improve collective labor processes.

The turning point from "yesterday" to "today" probably dates back to the beginning of 1923, when Rabkrin (Workers' and Peasants' Inspectorate) was reorganized. We shall discuss this issue in more detail later.

At this point we would like to dwell on reforms at Rabkrin in a more general way. These reforms were conceived as a response to current social trends. First and foremost, the revolution moved from the "critical" stage to the "organic" or construction stage. Accordingly, the focus of policy attention shifted to economics and engineering, including social engineering.

Social engineering as applied to everyday life moved to the top of the agenda following Trotsky's articles.

Lenin's earlier papers **(21)** that triggered reforms at Rabkrin and helped the NOT movement gain considerable momentum, were dealing with another aspect of social engineering, i.e., that of labor and cooperation as part of the culture of revolution at its "organic" stage.

Lenin did not treat improvements in government in terms of politics and economics only. He put this issue into a broader perspective of *the epoch* rather than *the current day.* He was concerned with the needs of the *practical culture of the revolution.* Hence his slogan "better fewer but better", his insistence on closer ties between Rabkrin and NOT, his appeal to engage in more "training" and so on. In any narrower context these ideas may seem incomprehensible if not burdensome.

"Our state apparatus is so deplorable, not to say wretched, that we must first think very carefully how to combat its defects, bearing in mind that these defects are rooted in the past, which, although it has been overthrown, has not yet been overcome, has not yet reached the stage of a culture, that has receded into the distant past. I say culture deliberately, because in these matters we can only regard as achieved what has become part and parcel of our culture, of our social life, our habits." ("Better Fewer But Better").

"In matters of culture, haste and sweeping measures are most harmful."

The last quote explains the point of "training" and the expediency of "combining educational activities (NOT) with official activities (Rabkrin)", "In all spheres of social, economic and political relationships we are "frightfully" revolutionary. But as regards precedence, the observance of the forms and rites of office management (that is, in the area of social engineering – N.V.) our "revolutionariness" often gives way to the mustiest routine. On more than one occasion, we have witnessed the very interesting phenomenon of a great leap forward in social life being accompanied by amazing timidity whenever the slightest changes are proposed. This is natural, for the boldest steps forward were taken in a field which was long reserved for theoretical study, which was promoted mainly, and even almost exclusively, in theory. ... Some great universal agrarian revolution was worked out with an audacity unexampled in any other country, and at the same time the imagination failed when it came to working out a tenth-rate reform in office routine; the imagination, or patience, was lacking to apply to this reform the general propositions that produced such "brilliant" results when applied to general problems." ("Better Fewer But Better").

Lenin conceived a reform that was not based on transient needs of today such as saving money on government. He raised a much broader issue, i.e., the use of social engineering to design and improve government agencies, and the use of scientific principles and scientific data in the struggle for a better culture of work and cooperation.

3. *NOT prospects in Russia*

How will Russian NOT develop in the future, what *areas* it will cover and what *methodology* it will employ?

Traditional NOT will face numerous surprises, especially in research and development.

In fact, traditional NOT is restricted to industry and cannot even imagine any other field of application. Industrial engineers are deemed to be its only possible agents.

This situation will certainly change. First, NOT itself has expanded already. Second, the organic stage of the revolution demands improvements in less explored areas of the economy; conversely, areas where NOT has been more active, will remain relatively dormant for a long time.

Traditional NOT has focused on large-scale industry. However, industrial development in Russia is inevitably slow, labor is cheap and competition among enterprises is non-existent. In this situation one can hardly expect any fast increase in grassroots initiatives to improve manufacturing processes. NOT, therefore, will have to concentrate on *administration* in government, industry and the army rather than on the actual factory shop. Administrative engineering, a relatively new field, will have to accommodate the emerging thrust of grassroots initiatives in the area of systematic scientific improvements.

Russian NOT has to start with issues that are the last ones for Western scientific management to address. This just confirms our belief, however, that NOT should primarily deal with *cooperation* as a matter of *social organization of labor* rather than simply *work;* that NOT's backbone is *social engineering;* that the true nature of NOT will be evident after the collapse of the individualistic capitalist culture, when it starts meeting the spontaneous demand for scientific control of social relations in everyday life, work and politics from the new collectivist culture.

The slow development of industry-oriented NOT is of course a purely Russian trait. It would hardly be possible, say, in Germany "the next day after a social upheaval." On the other hand, a high demand for NOT that concentrates on labor cooperation is inherent to cultural progress in any country including Russia.

Any social system creates a cooperation culture of its own. The Russian revolution expects NOT to help it forge a scientific approach to cooperation management.

4. Ways and means

Apart from focusing on new areas, NOT is also changing its structure and methodologies in response to the same social demand that has made it more active. We have already mentioned that the NOT of yesterday was an undifferentiated *ideological* trend combining research and practical improvements.

Now, as NOT institutions are growing and assuming an increasingly heavy workload, the movement has to become better organized, i.e., clearly separate theory and practice to avoid being crushed by the incredible burden of new challenges.

We have mentioned above that NOT will be challenged by life itself at the newest, most difficult and least fortified sector of the front line, i.e., the area of administrative engineering. This imminent attack calls for urgent capacity building in theoretical studies to lay a solid foundation for practical improvements and fight those traditionalists who will certainly find countless reasons to deny NOT the right to develop in this area. An appropriate methodology is also needed. These tasks require a well-run system dealing exclusively with theoretical research in administrative engineering.

Do not think that theoretical research prospers elsewhere at the NOT front. The situation there is fairly alarming. Foreign NOT as a system has obviously entered a period of crisis that cannot but spread to Russia. Indeed, even under the best of circumstances we would have had to initiate a crisis of traditional NOT ourselves. Any social science must

152

be fundamentally revised with a move to a different social system. Moreover, the revolution should inevitably turn the embryonic form of NOT into a full-fledged science.

Therefore, the traditional area of industrial NOT will also require a lot of hard theoretical work which, in turn, calls for drawing a clear border between research and practical improvements. These two areas should communicate rather than merge.

As for applied NOT, its development will necessarily be both intensive and extensive. This, again, requires that it should be separated from theoretical research.

Due to many ambiguous slogans and the lack of structural organization, the current practice of industrial improvements under the general banner of NOT has already led to much misunderstanding and thwarted the progress of our struggle for labor culture.

No doubt this struggle for labor culture and meaningful labor cooperation can be won by Soviet Russia only if the movement is 1) large-scale, 2) efficient and 3) based on *professional interest.*

Also, the success of NOT as the highest form of practical labor culture depends on broad and efficient grassroots support.

Of course, *a certain elementary labor culture must also be available as a starting point for progress.*

To sum up, the new period of struggle for practical labor culture involves a number of challenges that can be met only if NOT experts carefully separate their areas of responsibility.

5. *Organization*

An agency that is directly responsible for the labor culture campaign, the mobilization and coordination of appropriate forces and the systematic improvement of labor and cooperation techniques is the so called SOVNOT under the

People's Commissariat for the Workers' and Peasants' Inspectorate (PC for Rabkrin).

This representative center of institutions dealing with NOT and practical labor improvements also has a planning and coordinating function. It is a kind of a Revolutionary and Military Council for the labor culture campaign in Soviet Russia. Its tasks are very different from those of its parent organization SUIT (Labor Research Institutions Secretariat). SUIT has focused on research, methodological and ideological activities of NOT agencies rather than on promoting a broad campaign for practical improvements. In fact, this was quite natural for the *ideological* stage of NOT development in Russia.

The situation has changed radically, however. The All-Russian center for labor culture must – first and foremost – *actively promote systematic improvements in government agencies.* Of course, a reputable *NOT methodology center* is still needed more than ever, but methodology issues will be just one of the challenges (albeit probably the most important) faced by this center.

Let us try to outline these challenges to SOVNOT in the order of increasing difficulty:

1. Organizing a broad continuing education movement in the workforce.

Workers have already been showing keen interest in education. Lunacharsky **(22)** recently noted that the young generation is very much interested in *technology.* Trotsky makes the same observation in his "Issues of everyday life".

The spontaneous proliferation of various professional courses points to the same trend.

However, this spontaneous movement needs to be planned, organized and imbued with social spirit.

This work should primarily be done by trade unions and educational centers under the general guidance of SOVNOT. Every large organization should launch continuous education activities on a large scale.

2. Establishing a network of autonomous groups of narrow professionals dealing with improvements.

154

This step naturally follows the continuing education movement. It also means a transition to practical scientific improvements.

The broad continuing education campaign will identify the most active and skilled individuals such as lecturers, instructors and so on.

Such individuals should be given an opportunity to engage in improvement work as experts and consultants.

Once the systematic restructuring of government agencies gains momentum, these agencies will soon be in need of expert reviews, consultations and direct reconstruction services. We believe that private capitalism should be prevented from penetrating into this area by establishing appropriate non-government organizations that would unite professional accountants, office managers and administration experts.

3. Establishment of in-house improvement units in companies and agencies (pilot stations, organizational desks and so on).

The very first paragraph of the "Resolution by the All-Union Executive Committee and the Council of People's Commissars on the Reorganization of the People's Commissariat for the Workers' and Peasants' Inspectorate" states the following, "Heads of all government administrative and economic agencies will be held directly responsible to the state for the performance of said agencies.

The restructuring of government agencies to improve their performance must become an urgent task for every Soviet institution."

True responsibility and true efficiency are possible if two requirements are met: 1) the head of the agency should *know* his organization and its flaws in every detail; 2) a special department is available to deal with systematic restructuring and improvement.

Accordingly, 1) an in-house organization and control departments are needed and 2) they should include systematic improvement units (organizational desks or experimental stations).

155

4. In-house improvement work should be coordinated with supervision and guidance by the People's Commissariat for Rabkrin.

Practical improvements in offices and companies are supervised by organization and control departments. Centralized supervision is therefore also a must. Granted, no such government control of improvement work is known abroad. By the same token, however, foreign countries do not have a national economy that is entirely controlled by the government as we do. Therefore such structural differences with the West appear quite natural.

Whether the current forms of cooperation between SOVNOT (as a center for systematic labor and cooperation improvement) and Rabkrin are good or not, we have to admit that these two agencies need to maintain close ties.

5. Coordination between a) local improvement groups, b) corporate groups for systematic improvement and c) NOT research and development institutions. Aligning these three areas of work is the most difficult challenge faced by SOVNOT.

These areas need to be united under a single long-term plan of promoting labor culture.

The above outlines some general issues involved in the *organizational* activities of SOVNOT aimed at systematic improvement of labor and cooperation processes.

We should also mention another group of issues that relates to NOT *as such.*

They include a) coordination of NOT research, b) elaboration of general theories in various fields of NOT and c) teaching NOT.

These issues were addressed by SUIT. At the *ideological* stage of Russian NOT they were also subtly associated with the organization of applied NOT research.

Now that NOT is overcoming the stage of isolation from grassroots improvement initiatives and Soviet development needs scientific management to lead the long and difficult struggle for a new culture of labor and cooperation, NOT must radically change its organization.

As NOT was moving from its *ideological stage* to the *practical stage,* SUIT wanted to become a methodological center. This is a legitimate but a limited and rather self-contained goal. SOVNOT is not SUIT. A methodological center is just an element of a larger *organizational center* for systematic improvements in labor and cooperation techniques. If SOVNOT is the Revolutionary and Military Council of the struggle for labor culture in Soviet Russia, the methodological center is the Military Academy under the General Staff.

Again, research and practical improvements, while clearly separated, should be developing in tandem.

It will not be easy to turn SOVNOT into a true center of labor culture for *objective* as well as *subjective* reasons. The latter include primarily the attitudes that took shape at the ideological stage of Russian NOT. It is only logical, therefore, that bringing NOT closer to practice will not be easy, and finding best organizational arrangements for R&D in scientific management will take some time **(23)**.

2. N.A. Vitke, "Centre d'Etudes d'Administration"[71]

This center was established by Henri Fayol and his followers to advance administration research and improve current administration practices.

---

[71] This short article is reprinted unabridged from the magazine "Issues of Management and Administration" (*Voprosy organizatsii i upravleniya"*), 1925, No.3. As we have already mentioned above, orthodox Bolshevik NOT experts branded Vitke "a Russian Fayolist", which in their terms was an offensive and shameful name. "Fayolism or Marxism? E.F. Rozmirovich, Vitke's most ardent adversary, rhetorically asked in her paper under the same title. In the current paper, Vitke calmly explains to his opponents why Henri Fayol's school is worth attention and which of its theoretical and practical elements need not be arrogantly dismissed by Communist NOT experts in Soviet Russia.

It has three specific objectives:

1) *Collective development of administration science.*

Administration science has emerged from industrial as well as military practice.

It has gradually put forward a number of *empirical rules* to govern the behavior of human groups. The goal is to progress from these rules to genuine *laws of science* that would cover any human relations. Wherever humans compete or cooperate, they are subject to the same laws. Since administration science relates to any collective activities, be it at school, at a factory, in the army or in the trade union, it must move from the *rules* of industrial or military activity to *laws* of social life in general.

The collective development of administration science as a truly social discipline is the first objective of CEDA.

2) *The second objective is to address the flaws of today's education system* since its curriculum hardly includes any social practices. Fayolism insists that *elements of administration science should be taught to students at all levels of education.*

3) *The third objective of CEDA is to promote administration science and its achievements.*

Fayol's school calls itself a school of experimental administration. It is an important statement. It means that Fayolists study *real life* rather than ponder over some abstract ideal solutions. They do not aspire to establish some general principles as a basis for practical prescriptions. Quite the opposite, they use careful microscopic analysis of everyday activities, conduct experiments and systematize experience to grasp the laws that govern *actual life*. Reliable insights into the laws of collective human activities can be inferred only from a broad combination of practical experience and scientific experiments.

Is it at all possible to conduct these microscopic studies of social phenomena and the accumulation of billions of small facts from administration practice? Fayolism answers in the affirmative. In fact, social science has been using this methodology for quite a while. An enormous body of data has been collected and systematized. In particular, impressive progress in this field was made in France by Le Play **(24)** and his sociological school that meticulously studied the life of typical working class families. Various economic and sociological institutions have published a number of similar monographs dealing with rural communities, factories, Paris food organization and so on; the Ministry of Labor, the Defense Ministry and other government agencies also conducted such research. Some data were collected and systematized by the Social Museum as well as by the Scientific Management Society.

Accordingly, broad and detailed research into social phenomena is more than feasible. Moreover, an enormous wealth of available data in this field can be used and studied *from the standpoint of administration science.*

This research into data accumulated and systematized for other purposes is one of the areas on CEDA's agenda.

However, studying the literature is not the true focus of CEDA's work. Rather, it concentrates on the accumulation, systematization and analysis of the *current experience.* To this end CEDA has established an extensive network of *correspondents* who continuously supply data on present administrative practices, both on their own initiative and in response to CEDA's inquiries and questionnaires. The center analyzes, classifies and generalizes this evidence. Even facts that may seem trivial often hide intriguing aspects that can be discerned by a skillful analyst.

Henri Fayol's school believes in evidence-based analysis as the most appropriate methodology. Apart from general considerations pertinent to any science, it has its ideological leader as a role model. Indeed, Fayol developed the early framework of administration science precisely on the basis of meticulous accumulation of facts to gradually infer more general conclusions over the decades of his administrative career.

Like in nature at large, there can be no insignificant facts in human society. Every moment and every particular aspect reflects the whole, with all its diversity and general laws. This is why CEDA is so diligently recording and accumulating data on current administration practices.

Here is a collection of *pseudo-programs and pseudo-plans* that are useless at best. These are carelessly drafted without any regard for research or calculations, at somebody's own discretion. Even a small factory would never dare start a project based on such a pseudo-model. Even the most negligent architect would not dream of erecting a building according to such an impressionist plan. Yet we are still trying to organize hundreds of workers according to someone's sudden inspiration or as a matter of emergency. Such pseudo-plans may seem fairly detailed but they are developed single-handedly by a little czar of an administrator.

Here is a collection of ill-organized *meetings* that are convened unexpectedly or even at regular intervals but deal with emergencies rather than planned activities.

Here is a disorganized warehouse where goods are mechanically sorted by volume and weight without any attention to the current work, which causes a waste of time and labor.

Here is an unfortunate *administrator* who either does not know the personal qualities of his workers or consciously ignores them. Since the work environment he maintains does not relate to these qualities, it remains formal, cold and fruitless.

Here is an administrator who is lost in work details, struggling hard, incapable of following a policy, torturing himself and others by micro-management and dispersing his efforts instead of concentrating on his direct responsibilities.

Here is an administrator wary of more able subordinates who intentionally sows animosity among his workers to destroy the team spirit rather than reinforce it.

Here is an administrator who fails to realize that *any group of workers is held together by collective will.* What he sees is just a group of individuals. It does not occur to him that a team of people needs inspiration. He thinks emotions like work enthusiasm are irrelevant to business. The result is a tepid formal organization that consists of isolated units and cannot ensure an intense collective workflow.

Here is a useless *internal audit department* conceived as *an instrument of distrust.* It ignores some workers and focuses on others in emergencies rather than operates in a continuous and consistent fashion – and so on, and so forth.

To sum up, CEDA documents and systematizes a continuous flow of actual facts, organizes their collection in a certain order and in certain areas, analyzes and synthesizes them and checks its hypotheses against these facts. This hard work is slowly but surely contributing to the development of a consistent administration science.

3. E.F. Rozmirovich, On certain "scientific" management theories in government and industry[72]

I

Vladimir Ilich [Lenin] believed that Rabkrin (the Workers' and Peasants' Inspectorate) was meant to reform our government agencies on a sound scientific basis by rejecting the haphazard approach so typical of the past 5 years of countless government reforms that he dismisses it as "empty fuss." Instead, he put forward an objective of reforming our government by means of a long-term research based on the achievements of Western Europe and principles of NOT even if this work would take several years and yield no immediate tangible results.

It took the reformed Rabkrin quite a while to follow this recommendation, however. Its transition to scientific methodologies, timid and insecure at first, took hold both at

---

[72] This critical paper is a response to Vitke's book "Organization of Management and Industrial Development." The reader now has an opportunity to see how rude, improper and usually unfair was the criticism by this famous author serving the Kremlin. The paper is published unabridged from *The Socialist Economy (Sotsialisticheskoe khozyaistvo),* 1925, No.1.

Rabkrin and at government agencies that were implementing reforms after almost two years. At the same time, this transition became a mass movement, evoked enthusiastic response from government agencies, triggered broad publishing activity (original papers as well as translations) and put NOT at the focal point of all reform activities. We may say that Vladimir Ilich's objective and the course he suggested were well understood by the agencies concerned.

Nevertheless, an urgent and serious problem came up. Along with the methodology of NOT, implementation in our government agencies we had to analyze the very essence and contents of NOT principles from the standpoint of our proletarian state and its ideology. Also, as Marxists, we had to align these principles, which are claimed to be of scientific value, with the general theory of Marxism. Moreover, it was not clear whether the set of these principles could underlie a consistent science at all or they were doomed to be nothing more but a number of practical instructions for each industry and area of management. We feel obliged to draw the Party's attention to these theoretical issues that are currently being used to improve our government agencies, to this new section of the ideological front, especially because the situation here, like everywhere, suffers due to the lack of Party influence.

Abundant publications on these issues sell like hot cakes now because of the mass interest and the novelty of problems. Sometimes, however, this literature reflects a consistent philosophy that is based on impressive theories yet appears highly questionable. While methodologically wrong from the Marxist point of view, this philosophy is essentially void and useless if not outright harmful in practice. Nevertheless, it is presented to our workers in an apparently convincing and attractive format that employs Socialist rhetoric and quotes from Marx and Lenin, with authors claiming that the Soviet environment is much more favorable for its implementation than that in the bourgeois Europe.

The present paper will be limited to the analysis of just one such school, the so-called "Russian Fayolism" whose adepts support the theory of Henri Fayol, the French engineer. His Russian disciple N.A. Vitke has retold this theory "in his own words" for the USSR in a book called "Organization of

Management and Industrial Development" recently published for discussion by Rabkrin. In this book, whose second edition is to be published soon, the author consistently advocates exactly those anti-Marxist and unscientific views that we have just mentioned.

II

First of all, who is Fayol and how his theory applies to the bourgeois West, what social reasons gave rise to this theory, what is their true class content (no Marxist can be excused from asking this question while analyzing *any* social phenomenon) and what is its objective value from the working class perspective? We have to ask these questions and answer them before we move on to Russian Fayolists at least to be in a better position to fully describe and evaluate their position.

Fayol is the first Western European scholar who, as opposed to Taylor and others, attempts to promote and, to an extent, "scientifically" prove that a special science can and must be developed to deal with human management that should be consistently and consciously separated from the other parts of the more general field of enterprise management. Fayol divides all industrial operations into several groups such as technical, commercial, financial operations and so on, and singles out their specific administration function. Each of these operations, he holds, requires a certain "skill" that, in turn, needs a special set of individual psychological qualities from its bearer. As Fayol raises the issue of the need in a special administration science, he focuses on this function as a matter of special research and defines it exclusively as "the art to handle people". "Administrative functions, - he writes, - are an organ and a tool of a social structure; while other functions (commercial, financial and the like – E.R.) deal with materials and machines, administrative functions affect people only." (Fayol, *"General and Industrial Management"*, published by the Central Institute of Labor, p. 24).

In Vitke's account, the administration function is "to intentionally influence personnel in work collectives in order to establish a harmonious unity of members, stimulate individual and collective performance, and concentrate scattered wills in a certain single direction." (Ibid., p.102). Such "consistent leadership and influence on workers", Vitke maintains, are required due to modern industrial development; this "organizational and administrative influence" should be based on "sound scientific knowledge and meticulous research" and be "comprehensive, continuous, plan-based and strictly methodological." (Ibid.)

No special kind of vision is needed to see the true class meaning behind these pompous phrases. The objective (at least in the West according to Fayol) is to teach modern industrial administrators to manage *workers* (as opposed to factories as a whole) in such a way that they would maintain a harmonious unity of all parts of the work collective, have a maximum individual and collective productivity and concentrate their "wills" in a certain direction strictly specified by the entrepreneur. All this is achieved by developing a special science concerning "such" management and based on "sound scientific knowledge and meticulous research." Further on, Fayol's school shows similar diligence in studying the specific psychological qualities required from an administrator to master *the art of handling people* (persistence, restraint, willpower and so on) and the objective means that can help achieve "the concentration of wills" by workers themselves (profit sharing, etc.). Vitke believes that the new school is fundamentally different from older ones because it puts special emphasis on "social organization" issues that Taylor did not distinguish from general management problems. Also, the new school regards the worker as a social and psychological individual, whereas "Taylor thought of the worker as an element of production similar to materials and tools". (Ibid., p.123).

This is the ideological and political essence of Fayolism. No doubt that in terms of class struggle in the West it is yet another attempt (this time using "scientific methods") to organize the exploitation of workers in such a way that all their "wills" (or aspirations – E.R.) would be diverted from the objectives of class struggle to benefit the entrepreneur, i.e., directed towards absolute obedience to his orders aimed at further exploitation and profit-making. For conditions in the West we can offer no other opinion; moreover, it is the only opinion that should be expressed by any true Marxist prior to evaluating this theory for some other purposes. Unfortunately, we could not find this assessment in citizen Vitke's book; quite the opposite, we found praise for the activities of "administrative staffs" at capitalist factories in the West that are engaged in "systematic research" and "planned guidance" of "all issues related to personnel and the stimulation of collective labor." (Ibid., p.103).

The International Congress on Management in Prague provided a wealth of material to understand the true nature and sources of this problem and the "administration science" created by Fayol and now upheld by Vitke. One of the prominent issues at the congress was how the worker's psyche can be subdued to the entrepreneur and how the worker can be made to toil meekly for the capitalist. It was raised either as analysis of the "social factor in scientific management" or the issue of "personal relations in industry" or, finally, as that of "relations between labor and capital in the US and Czechoslovak industry." We shall give a few typical quotes from one of the presentations on this issue, namely Dr. Link's report "On individual relations in industry".

"The objective of any industry," he starts, "is to satisfy human needs." Any individual, "whether a worker or a capitalist" seeks to "satisfy his immediate needs, while the welfare of society ranks second". "This leads", Link continues, "to discontent among the working masses, frequent strikes and sabotage, as well as to the establishment of trade unions and other organizations by means of which workers hope to achieve welfare they cannot reach as individuals." Sometimes, "labor unions become powerful enough to dictate their will to factory owners." "Through *bitter and often expensive experience* (italics are mine – E.R.)", he observes, "the businessman concludes that he is not capable of fully meeting his own needs without making *major concessions to the needs and welfare* of his partners and employees." As a result, capitalists come to "better realize the value of an individual and better understand that all the advantages of scientific control over materials and mechanical processes would be available only to a limited extent without voluntary interest from employees and close cooperation with the working masses."

He goes on to say that "It has become clear that all these activities (attempts at solving "the problem of human nature in industry" – E.R.) had a single objective, i.e., to create a loyal, intelligent and satisfied (with its situation – E.R.) personnel." To this end, personnel administration departments were set up as well as learned societies, particularly the prominent American Management Association that deals entirely with this human problem. It is significant that Vitke refers to these American experts and their work as a model for professional administrators (whom he promotes) without any critical remarks. At present, we are not interested in the reasons for the absence of such remarks. We have a more important problem right now.

Since Fayolism claims to be a science in terms of its subject as well as methodology, our author, on the one hand, associates it with a number of mainstream disciplines such as physiology, reflexology and objective psychology. On the other hand, he tries to validate his own claims (for the USSR, because they are not credible for the West anyway) by referring to our Marxist ideas on the evolution of capital and economic relations in general as well as to our Communist concepts of the future social order. In fact, he tries to prove that the principles of "personnel management" that he advocates are broadly identical to our Communist principles.

We should discuss this theory in earnest, take up the challenge from the author across the board and refute his ideas concerning the static and dynamic relationship between the psychological and the industrial factor at a modern enterprise. We should take a look at his concept of types of social relations, specifically the forms of management in the proletarian state of the future; finally, we should check his quotes from Marx and Lenin, the founders and leaders of revolutionary Marxism, since he tries to use these quotes as theoretical support for his erroneous and practically harmful conclusions.

III

Let us start from the section of the book where Vitke presents the history of the new school and makes an effort to provide objective reasons for the inevitable inception of the school itself as well as its subject, i.e., the "management problem" as a matter of scientific research. In fact, if we demonstrate that no such subject exists or that it emerged for no particular reason or, at least, that there are no special reasons to study it in the USSR, this would be sufficient to make all his other assumptions completely irrelevant or, in any case, not worth a rebuttal.

Let us follow the author now.

"NOT comes from the same cradle", Vitke writes, "as all the other broad cultural movement of today such as modern technology, modern science and modern scientific socialism, that is, from *industry*. It was the metal industry that gave birth to Taylorism and Fordism. Moreover, both theories emerged during the period of its intense and rapid concentration and cartelization late in the 19th century. The "broad NOT" of the French school of experimental administration led by the engineer Fayol who challenged government administration, the army, trade, educational, political, and other social management systems to "industrialize" is also rooted in industry." (Ibid., p.5).

So far the author is perfectly right. Capitalism in general and large-scale industrialism in particular have extremely aggravated the forms of class struggle, put on the agenda the "human problem" as presented by Link at the Prague Congress, and forced Fayol and others to put forth the "administration problem" as a task of "conquering and concentrating the wills of workers." Our author, however, tries to use *this fact* to deduce something more significant, namely, a kind of an objective and immanent "law".

"... from spontaneous everyday practices", he writes, "in the atmosphere of fierce competition ... a special *profession* (italics added– E.R.) of management consultants has gradually emerged... and large firms are established to deal with this business." (Ibid., p.15). Elsewhere he claims that "as this function becomes more independent and professional in larger and more complex [industrial – E.R.] organizations, it requires independent *professional managers and administrators.*" (Ibid., p.11). Finally, he writes that "This process of concentration ... generates a unique *professional* group of hired managers." (Ibid., p. 9.)

The author believes, therefore, that the emergence of this group of specialists as a distinct social category of administrators is largely *an inevitable manifestation* of social relations generated by the production process and *inherent* to this process. It is claimed to be a truly *objective fact* that needs to be taken into account, something quite different from Link's concept.

Is it really the case, however? Is it true that industrial development and concentration of manufacturing at giant factories bring to life a distinct group of professional administrators who are allegedly indispensable for the production process? Is it right to attribute to it such an inseparable link to the production process? How much sense does it make to claim that these professional organizers and administrators have a function of handling people and their aspirations, and that there is no other *force* determining the direction of these aspirations in the production process, a force of a very different nature and origin that the author ignores?

These issues, as you see, are so fundamental and deep that we are entitled to ask our author for evidence that would be more compelling than a mere referral to some groups that have appeared in England or will presumably appear in the course of time. More definitive proof is needed to postulate an objective economic law.

The author tries hard to provide such proof. He ignores arguments by Link and his like-minded colleagues and does not even mention them. He is certainly right, since the emergence of Link's engineers as a group (here Vitke would agree) can in no way be *objectively associated* with the production process as such (like the emergence of wholesale buyers during the transition from artisanal production to manufactures or that of the worker as a special element of the production process with the inception of factories). Our author has yet to demonstrate that his group of professional administrators has an objective function necessary for production.

"Industrialism is essentially based on machinery", Vitke writes, "A large-scale enterprise must use state-of-the-art machines." (Ibid., p. 22). "*Organizational* work is just as vital to industrialism as *machine design,*" since "a machine in itself is *blind and dead.* Its potential can fully materialize only as a result of *sound human (social and industrial) organization.* Therefore industrialism raises several unique new *organizational* issues to be addressed in large-scale production." (Ibid., italics added – E.R.).

This is the focal point of Vitke's delusions. Let us dwell on it in more detail. "In this area, the modern world faces a major challenge, - Vitke continues on p.24, - that disarms an engineer completely and has to be tackled by new professionals, the *organizers.*" So, the heart of the matter is that a large factory has gathered throngs of people around machinery and now its management is facing an organizational problem, i.e., the question of how these people should be governed, how to make them breathe life into dead machinery, how to build such a social-industrial (in Vitke's terms) *human* organization that would be willing and capable (concentration of aspirations) to use these dead and blind machines to their full capacity. According to Vitke, the production process triggered this problem in the capitalist society and, in order to solve it, gave rise to a special group of professional organizers, along with the group of engineers and design engineers who were unable to address it.

This is how Vitke justifies the presumed connection between this group and the production process. As additional proof, he happens to quote... Das Kapital by Marx. Well, let us turn to Marx's evidence invoked by Vitke.

"Since the fractional product of each detail laborer is, at the same time, only a particular stage in the development of one and the same finished article, each laborer, or each group of laborers, prepares the raw material for another laborer or group. The result of the labor of the one is the starting-point for the labor of the other. The labor-time necessary in each partial process for attaining the desired effect is learned by experience; and the mechanism of Manufacture, as a whole, is based on the assumption that a given result will be obtained at a given time." "It is clear that this direct dependence of the operations, and therefore of the laborers, on each other, compels each one of them to spend on his work no more than the necessary time, and thus a continuity, uniformity, regularity, order, and even intensity of labor, of quite a different kind, is begotten that is to be found in an independent handicraft or even in simple cooperation." "The division of labor, as carried out in Manufacture, not only simplifies and multiplies the qualitatively different parts of the social collective laborer but also creates a fixed mathematical relation or ratio, which regulates the quantitative extent of those parts, i.e., the relative number of laborers or the relative size of the group of laborers for each detail operation."

According to Marx, technical division of labor plays an even greater role in large-scale industry. As Vitke also quotes, "modern industry has a productive organism that is purely objective, in which the laborer becomes a mere appendage to an already existing material condition of production" where *"machinery operates only by means of associated labor, or labor in common."* Therefore, *"the cooperative character of the labor-process is, in the latter case, becomes a technical necessity dictated by the instrument of labor itself."* (Italics by Vitke – E.R.).

Based on these quotes and the fact that the "cooperative" nature of associated labor is evident even during the manufacture period, the author believes that he has proven the objective necessity of his special group of organizers who should help workers bring dead machinery to life, realize this "cooperative nature" and establish a special "social-production human organization" for collective work.

Most unfortunately, the author actually proves exactly the opposite. By quoting Marx he demonstrates that in simple cooperation, and even more so in manufacture, as hunger, misery, violence, and coercion were driving workers into factories and forced them to sell their labor, it was *manufacturing technology, i.e., the dead machinery* that played the organizing role due to which, as Marx put it, "the various supplementary labor-processes can proceed uninterruptedly, simultaneously, and side by side." Moreover, the direct dependence of the operations, and therefore of the laborers, on each other, compels each one of them to spend on his work no more than the necessary time, which created "a fixed mathematical relation or ratio which regulates the quantitative extent of those parts, i.e., the relative number of laborers, or the relative size of the group of laborers, for each detail operation." In other words, the author demonstrates that in the absence of administration experts (who merely did not exist at that time) who are supposed to breathe life into machines, these dead machines themselves created certain relations between workers in time and space and therefore established *a sound social-production human organization without any such experts.* So our author proves something exactly opposite to his point.

Marx applied this idea to an even greater extent to machine production, "a productive organism that is purely objective, in which the laborer becomes a mere appendage to an already existing material condition of production". Accordingly, in a situation where work is impossible without mass cooperation, there is no particular need for the industrial worker to understand the cooperative nature of labor and no need in professional administrators.

Our author, however, believes that he has already substantiated the need for such special group of organizers and goes even further. "Organization of an integrated production process by thousands of detail workers with dissimilar skills on the basis of a continuous manufacturing flow and maximum coordination among all members of the production chain is a task brought to the top of the agenda by the process of industrial development." (p.27). "However, the organizational revolution in large-scale manufacturing is much broader," continues Vitke on p.54, "*It affects not only relations among things and relations between things and humans but also relations among people involved in the industrial production process.*" He believes that "the entire art and the entire objective of management" is 1) "to provide a concrete system of manufacturing tasks for each of these groups and subgroups", 2) "to supply all the necessary instructions and materials to fulfill these tasks, and, finally, 3) "to allow as much freedom as possible to the executor, induce and continuously maintain the group's interest in the best execution of the task." The last objective is met as the new system "makes a direct effect on production relations ("the objective manufacturing organism of the enterprise")   and *simultaneously fosters "the spirit of the hive", i.e., interest in the outcome of work from every team and the entire collective."* (Ibid, p. 56). Vitke claims to describe the specific *production function* that is indispensable to the industrial process that has brought to life the group of professional organizers and put the "management issue" on the agenda.

"Rather than being an engineer or technician, the modern organizer and administrator is primarily a social builder, a unifier, and director of human wills. Human resources are much more important to him than the issues of technology... A modern administrator is largely a constructor of human relations." (Ibid., p.61). [The] special *administrative function* ... [is] *a unique social profession aimed at appropriately uniting and guiding collective work efforts* (p. 63). "The administrator's core job is to ignite and sustain ownership and work enthusiasm. He must be a *born leader* in whatever area, be it even the manufacturing and distribution of shoe polish. (Ibid., p.91, italics added – E.R.).

These are the concepts elaborated by the author and this is how he interprets the functions of his group and his administration science. The sore point is still there, however. Namely, *is the emergence of this group of administrators associated with the objective development of the production process?* We found no answer to this question save for some general phraseology concerning the cooperative role of the labor process. Vitke's statements, as we have established, do not apply to the manufacture period. He does not want to associate this necessity with Link's interpretation of the group in question. The only opportunity left to us is to give an answer ourselves by analyzing the objective modern production process at its two stages, (a) in the bourgeois capitalist society and (b) in the socialist society. We shall thus clearly see the scientific, political and practical value of all this admiration for "professional administrators" as well as all the philosophical, psychological and economic theories promoted by N. Vitke.

IV

Does the production process in the developed capitalist society in the bourgeois West need those "professional administrators" and "organizers of wills"? Let us turn to the famous Ford factory as something typical of large-scale industrialism and see how the production process is organized there. This time, however, we shall give the floor to Comrade Bukharin **(26)** rather than Vitke. This is what he writes:

"If, as an example of a capitalist enterprise, we take Mr. Ford's automobile factory in Detroit; its emphatically modern character is the first trait to strike the eye: a precise division of labor, much machinery, operating automatically under the supervision of the workers, strict adherence to a correct succession of operations, etc. Parts of the product are carried along by slowly moving belts or platforms, and the various types of workers at their machines execute their specific tasks on the partly finished articles as they go by. The entire labor process has been calculated down to the second. Each displacement of the worker, each motion of hand or foot, each inclination of the body, all have been foreseen. The "staff" supervises the general course of the work; everything goes by the clock, or rather, the chronometer. Such is the division of labor and its "scientific organization" according to the Taylor system. Such a factory, if we consider its human structure, i.e., the relations between the individuals composing it, also constitutes a productive relation, in which the distribution of persons and their relation with each other are determined by the system of machinery, the combinations of machines, the technology, and the organization of the factory inventory." ("Voprosy sovetskogo khozyaistva i upravleniya", No. 4-5, 1924. E. Rozmirovich, "Results of Rabkrin work on NOT" *(K itogam raboty RKI po NOT)*, p. 116). We have already used this quote in an argument against the same author. We shall take the liberty of exactly quoting our own words that followed it:

"What kind of control over human relations during the production process could be possibly exercised by our author at such a factory? What kind of science and what kind of administration could we talk about? Everything here is taken into account, brought under control and foreseen. This collective needs no administration or leadership. Machinery rules in this case, the administrator is nothing but a technician." A bit earlier in the same paper we made another comment on the same issue: "Mechanization in manufacturing eventually leads to mechanization in management and reduces it to mechanical supervision that leaves no room for management in the old sense of the word as a specific command function. This is the ultimate outcome of industrial development. The sum of technical knowledge along this process turns exclusively into that concerning production technology and the laws of the work process, while administration turns into supervision over this process."

We still fully agree with these words and challenge our author to contest them (of course, without resorting to Link's arguments who claims that "without workers' interest in the success of production", that is, without arresting the class struggle altogether, all NOT methods will hardly give any results. Earlier, however, we agreed to disregard Link's theories, since what we are discussing now is the alleged connection between the production process and the objective need in a special group of professional administrators dictated by the production process itself.

We have found no such connection even in the capitalist society. Moreover, it is evident that its development hardly makes the role of these administrators any stronger. Quite the opposite, the very administration function appears to be on its way to extinction and complete replacement by relations between machines that will ultimately define everything at the factory including the direction of human wills.

Bukharin wrote more on this subject in his collection "The Attack" (p. 120-121). "Bogdanov **(27)** believes that even machines should be regarded not as things but rather as the human ability to work with certain tools as a result of psychological training. This psychological Marxism clearly

174

deviates from the principle of materialism in sociology that Marx emphasized." He goes on to say, "I understand productive relations as labor coordination between people (viewed as live machines) in space and time. This system is hardly any more psychological than the Solar system with its planets. A system is defined by the fact that any of its parts have a certain position at any given moment. From this point of view there is no room for psychology in the basis. This, I believe, is the only possible and the only materialistic solution."

Bukharin's words were said in connection with a different matter. Yet they deal a blow to Vitke's "psychological" arguments and become particularly relevant in the light of experiments performed by Comrade Gastev, Vitke's opponent, in his Institute of Labor. According to Gastev, the social engineer is not an organizer. Rather, he is a machine whose design and actions define *the psychological reactions of the live worker and make these reactions merge with the system of mechanisms to form integrated systems of machine motions.* Sophisticated machine tools in this case directly define or evoke reactions that become so spontaneous as to completely *switch off the individual conscience of the worker,* the source of energy that, once free, can be used by the worker for other purposes.

In terms of the general theory of Marxism and the true prospects of industrial development, Gastev evidently takes a more scientific and realistic position than Vitke. The theory proposed by Gastev (which is quite acceptable for Marxists and has a true scientific content) is a forward-looking system that opens endless prospects for further improvement. In comparison to these prospects, Vitke's theory seems like a pathetic repetition of socialist revolutionary fantasies and old idealistic nonsense. Therefore, we can now be certain that even in the modern bourgeois capitalist society there is no *objective* connection between industrial progress and the need for a special group of "will organizers" to direct the production process. Moreover, industrial progress tends to *eliminate the administration function in production completely.*

In essence, there is not much more to say. We have demonstrated that a special administration science as interpreted by Vitke is becoming irrelevant and even unfeasible, since the center defining human behavior shifts from the "psychological influence by the professional administrator" to machinery. Since Vitke uses his theory of the objective role of these administrators in the production process as a starting point to develop a number of equally erroneous concepts concerning the role of these administrators in the future society and the structure of this society, however, we feel obliged to deal with this theory at a somewhat greater length in order to completely expose its unscientific, inconsistent, anti-Marxist and counterrevolutionary nature.

V

Let us now discuss how Russian Fayolists view the structure of the future socialist society as well as the issues of practical work in today's Soviet Russia.

"The administration science," Vitke writes, "dealing with the progress of labor collectives under capitalist industrialism is only capable of handling particular issues and yielding partial results." (p. 127). It is only under socialism that *the administration science can expand to become a cultural transformation force of as much scope and significance as natural sciences* that now enjoy unlimited opportunities for development." (p. 128, italics added – E.R.). Accordingly, the new school will act as a cultural transformation force at least as powerful as natural sciences. Its members will teach culture and promote new ideas in whose absence the new society would be incapable of addressing its problems.

"NOT will be able to develop completely only on the basis of social and economic prerequisites of socialism – and vice versa. *The socialist economy will be able to advance only on the basis of administration of sophisticated and differentiated labor collectives.*" (Italics added – E.R.) Vitke believes that our revolutionary leaders agree with these prospects and have therefore emphasized the importance of NOT.

"First comes electrification as the technological basis of socialism, followed by NOT as its organizational basis. This

176

sequence is not accidental. It is an interconnected chain of events that serves as a foundation for *further opportunities* of building socialism." (The italics are mine – E.R.) The author predicts that "NOT work will not focus on production, or at least not on factory shops. Mainstream NOT research will concentrate on *administration issues in the government, the economy, the army and industry*" (p.140, the italics are mine – E.R.), or, as he puts it later on the same page, "in everyday life, in work, in political life". (Italics added – E.R.)

It is interesting to note that Vitke is hardly an innovator. His teacher Fayol has similar dreams about France and bourgeois Europe at large, with some modifications made for capitalist rather than socialist productive relations.

Both at the International Social Sciences Congress in Brussels (1923) and in his book "General and Industrial Management" Fayol criticized the existing parliamentary democracy for not meeting *the basics of scientific administration.* These basics require continuity and specialization, whereas the parliamentary system leads to incessant changes in government and demise of ministries.

"We know the importance of forecasting at a large enterprise; what it requires from management is professional competence, experience, administration skills, energy, moral courage and so on. We come across this set of qualities at most large French enterprises. As for governance in France, reports from parliament indicate that this is not the case. ... Transient ministers have no time to acquire professional competence, experience and administration skills needed to develop an action plan. Eloquence, undeniably an indispensable quality for a minister, cannot substitute knowledge that is accumulated over a certain period of time in the process of practical work and the exercise of power. Naturally, there must be some *stability of office.* Ministerial instability is a national disaster..."

"Another reason the current government is so inept is the lack of managerial responsibility... A remedy, again, is *stability of tenure* that connects the minister to his office and imparts moral strength – the only true guarantee wherever management of excessively large enterprises is concerned... (Fayol, pp. 61-62, the italics are mine – E.R.).

Hence the slogan "to industrialize politics", i.e., transplant industrial management practices (with experts, designers and administrators) to political life and government. This slogan proposed by Fayol's school is *ideologically related* to Vitke's claims. In both cases it is assumed that the future *forms* and *practical methods* of government depend on the handling of the *"mainstream administration problem"*, as our author puts it, "in government, the economy, the army and industry [...] in everyday life, work and political life" with the help of their allies, the teachers of the new society.

It is already clear that these claims are incompatible with the fundamental principles of our government system and our civil society. These principles include the election of all civil servants, the possibility of their recall at any time by the electorate (the Soviets) and, finally, the organization of government in such a way that *any kitchen maid would be able to run the country and every single worker would take turns to do government work.* These principles were put forward on the basis of precise scientific forecasts of the inevitable objective evolution of industrial development and social relations after the expropriation of bourgeoisie. These principles continue to determine our practical policies and hardly agree with the idea of a distinct group of professional administrators that will have a special role in the future. On the other hand, these ideas run contrary to all our concepts about the future state.

Let us remind you Vladimir Ilich's [Lenin] words. "The development of capitalism, in turn, creates the preconditions that enable really "all" to take part in the administration of the state. Some of these preconditions are: universal literacy, which has already been achieved in a number of the most advanced capitalist countries, then the "training and disciplining" of millions of workers by the huge, complex, socialized apparatus of the postal service, railways, big factories, large-scale commerce, banking, etc., etc." ("State and Revolution", "Moskovskiy Rabochiy Publishers", p. 86).

Accordingly, Vladimir Ilich suggested *technology* rather than some "mainstream administration" as a powerful means of *teaching* workers to run the state, of *simplifying* the administration of the state and, finally, as a major factor of "not only *bringing the broad masses closer to government but also*

178

the eventual elimination of government." This concept was bequeathed to us as a theoretical system and as a *practical slogan.* "This beginning [of the socialist revolution – E.R.] on the basis of large-scale manufacturing," Vladimir Ilich continues, "gradually evolves into a system where the *ever simplifying functions* of supervision and accounting will be performed *by everyone in turn,* will become a *habit and will finally disappear as special functions of special people."* (Ibid., p.40, italics added – E.R.).

The future portrayed here by Vladimir Ilich certainly in no way agrees with Vitke's concepts or with his interpretation of the driving forces that will lead to this future. Instead of a state where *everybody governs* so that the government itself *disappears as a function,* instead of "training and disciplining" of workers by the production process itself to foster such system of running the state, instead of the Marxist idea that *the progress of technology* is the main engine of development he suggests that no socialist development is possible whatsoever without the organizational and administrative activities of the above group, that these activities will inevitably extend to "everyday life, work and politics", Fayolists also believe that administration is a much more important field for research and development than technology, since "NOT work will not concentrate on factory shops".

Suffice it to say that a deep abyss separates these theories from Marxism and Leninism.

Finally, what would be *the practical value* of these concepts if they were to be officially endorsed or implemented?

The new school of Fayolism *has not given and cannot give anything practical.* Our author also could not provide any practical recommendations apart from general phrases about "cultivating the spirit of the hive" and creating some special "socio-psychological atmosphere". Objectively speaking, he could do little more, because real life turned out to be controlled and governed by factors entirely different from those that were claimed to exist and need cultivation by Fayol, Vitke and their followers.

Part III. Notes and comments

(1) Let us expand somewhat on Vitke's brief outline of NOT history in Soviet Russia. The First All-Russian Conference in January 1921 sparked a broad movement for scientific management in various organizational forms[73] divided by Vitke into five basic categories:

1) research institutes and laboratories,

2) ministerial agencies,

3) practical innovation units at enterprises and factories,

4) non-governmental organizations,

5) central administration and coordination agency for the entire movement.

The *leading research institutes* were TsIT (The Central Labor Institute, headed by A.K. Gastev), KINOT (The Kazan Scientific Management Institute, headed by I.M. Burdyanskiy), the Ukrainian Labor Institute (headed by F.R. Dunaevskiy), TINOP (The Taganrog Scientific Industrial Management Institute, headed by P.M. Yesmanskiy), GITU (The State

---

[73] See: NOT in the USSR. A Reference Book. *[NOT v SSSR: Spravochnik.]* Moscow, 1924; Kerzhentsev P.M., NOT: Scientific Management and Objectives of the Party. *[NOT: Nauchnaya organizatsiya truda i zadachi partii.]* Moscow-Peterburg, 1923; Deyneko O.A., Scientific Management in the USSR. *[Nauka upravleniya v SSSR].* Moscow, 1967; Berkovich D.M., A Brief History of Scientific Management in Industry. *[Formirovanie nauki upravleniya proizvodstvom: Kratkiy istoricheskiy ocherk.]* Moscow, 1973; Lavrikov Yu.A. and Koritskiy E.B., Issues in the Development of Socialist Scientific Management. *[Problemy razvitiya teorii upravleniya sotsialisticheskim proizvodstvom.]* 2nd edition. Leningrad, 1989.

Institute of Administration Technology under PC RKI, headed by E.F. Rozmirovich) and a few others. These institutes focused on the development of theoretical ideas and systematic concepts based on research into management practices. Since field work was an integral part of this process, the most advanced scholars could not afford staying in their labs and offices. They wanted to combine academic studies with practice, and the majority of research centers at that time also dealt with practical innovation. Not all of these attempts were equally successful yet the experience of for-profit consulting agencies such as "Ustanovka" ("Setup") under TsIt, ITU's "Orgstroy" and others is still of considerable interest today.

Apart from research and work improvement many leading institutes were also involved in training of administrators at various levels. These included, among others, TsIT, ITU, KINOT, TINOP and a number of colleges and engineering schools. Professor Monroy from Germany noted in TsIT's guestbook that "Such a combination of a *research* and *educational* institution as yet does not exist in Western Europe."[74]

The combination of research, practical innovation and training was one of the most valuable approaches developed during the 1920s, since this "triune" mechanism is the core for the development of scientific management.

Research into scientific management was also pursued, albeit on a smaller scale, by *ministerial agencies with a consulting function.*

They included, among others, the Initiative Commission on Industrial Scientific Management under the Council of Ministers set up in 1920 and reorganized into the Scientific Management Division in 1920; The Central Industrial Management Bureau under the War Industry Department of the Council of Ministers (1921); the NOT division of the Chief

---

[74] Glushkov V.M., Dobrov G.M., Tereshchenko V.I., Conversations about management. *[Besedy ob upravlenii].* MOSCOW, 1974. P. 191.

Engineering Committee (1920), and the Special Commission on Scientific Management in Transportation (TsNORT, 1923, reorganized and renamed the NOT division of the Planning Department, 1924) under the Ministry of Railways. Consulting agencies and practical innovation offices were also ubiquitous at that time.

As opposed to institutes and laboratories, such organizations focused primarily on practical applications. After conducting reviews of factories in various industries, they used NOT principles to streamline operations and management. While certainly relying on the concepts developed by institutes and laboratories, this practical work also spawned its own theories of general relevance for the economy.

Practical innovation divisions at specificities and enterprises such as pilot stations, orga-stations, organization bureaus, practical innovation bureaus and special self-financing trusts played a special role in the NOT movement. Relatively little has been written about these entities in literature though they were responsible for most practical innovation efforts in work and management.

In a situation where "senior management enthuses over modern innovation ideas, while lower organizations are wallowing in the swamp of purely Russian technological and cultural backwardness,"[75] these bodies actually "ignited and encouraged innovation and restructuring efforts."[76] They were also the main source of data to be systematized by research institutes developing "the organizational science."[77]

The development of these units was thwarted with the lack of financing, a shortage of experts in practical innovation (for clear reasons) and the occasional misinterpretation of

---

[75] Goltsman A.Z., At the threshold of innovation. [*U poroga ratsionalizatsii.*] "Khozyaistvo i upravlenie", 1926, No.3. P. 13.

[76] "Za Ratsionalitsiyu", 1928, №8. C. 11.

[77] Rozmirovich E., "Present and Future Status of Orgbureaus at Government Agencies" *[Sovremennoe sostoyanie i perspektivy rabot orgbyuro v gosudarstvennykh uchrezhdeniyakh.]* "Tekhnika upravleniya", 1925, No.4. P. 4.

their functions by senior management. Nevertheless, it should be admitted that the establishment of dedicated innovation units at every level, (from factories, groups of companies, and ministries to the very Council of Ministers) was an utterly sound idea.

A variety of *non-governmental organizations* such as the Time League (later renamed the NOT League) and its cells, NOT workshops, factory innovation groups and RKI assistance groups also appeared due to public interest in scientific management. P.M. Kerzhentsev, chairman of the Time League, believed that tangible results can be expected only "if we stimulate interest in NOT in broad working masses and engage them in active NOT work."[78] Of course, he continued, progress in scientific management does need research institutes and laboratories, but grassroots organizations are also important because they "support and enhance research and development."[79]

Established in 1923, the Time League quickly expanded its ranks to tens of thousands of members across the country and effectively became the grassroots wing of the NOT movement. Later it was renamed the NOT League whose founders, apart from Kerzhentsev, included famous NOT scholars such as I.N. Shpilreyn, I.A. Zalkind, M.P. Rudakov and A.M. Kaktyn.[80]

Finally, a few words about the fifth component of NOT efforts in Russia. The First All-Russian NOT Conference proposed a unified national agency that would "coordinate research of all scientific centers in the Republic that can contribute to a powerful science of management and develop practical methods of executing Soviet economic plans."[81] S.

---

78 Kerzhentsev P.M., NOT at the Economic Front. [*NOT na khozyaystvennom fronte.*] "Vremya", 1924, No.4. P. 4.

[79] Ibid.

[80] Kerzhentsev P.M., Principles of Organization. [*Printsipy organizatsii*]. Moscow, 1968. P. 453.

[81] Proc. of the First All-Russian Conference on Scientific Organization of Labor and Production, January 20-27, 1921. [Trudy 1-i Vserossiyskoy Initsiativnoy konferentsii po

Rayetskiy, who suggested the idea, wanted the new body to be called "The State Institute of Social Mechanics and Psychophysiology of Labor." A report was unanimously endorsed by all delegates and sent to STO ("The Council for Labor and Defense"); it suggested that the proposed Bureau for the Scientific Management of Labor and Production under STO would develop a program for research institutes and other organizations.[82] The conference also elected members of the Secretariat for Labor Research Institutes (SUIT) that was instructed to consolidate the NOT movement in the country. The Kremlin, especially Lenin, however, was not impressed, since Bolsheviks believed in total centralization of every single aspect of life and wanted the proposed national authority to be more powerful. As is well-known, Lenin proposed that the Workers' and Peasants' Inspectorate be merged with the Party's Central Control Commission to monitor and lead the entire NOT movement in the country.

The XII Congress of the Russian Communist Party in April 1923 endorsed this idea and established a new RKI-CCC agency headed by Kuybyshev. Vitke, as you may remember, was appointed chief of the Standardization Division (later called the Administration Technology Division) for this key agency. As evidenced by A.K. Gastev, reforms in government agencies started in earnest only once this division was set up. In fact, he calls it "the most valuable, active and creative part of the governance reforms department at RKI."[83]

Also, a Scientific Management Council (SOVNOT) was established at RKI to coordinate and plan all NOT-related activities by institutes, laboratories, associations and NGOs. The task, however, turned out to be beyond the strength of a single agency, and in November 1926 SOVNOT was closed down.

Nauchnoy Organizatsii Truda i Proizvodstva 20-27 yanvarya 1921 goda]. V.6, Moscow, 1921. P. 16.

[82] Ibid., p. 8.

[83] See: Scherbakovskiy G.Z., Scientific Management in Russia: World-class Schools and Scholars. Book 1. "A.K.Gastev and TsIT", Frankfurt-am-Main, 2014, P. 129-130.

These are the main organizational forms of the NOT movement in the USSR in the 1920s.

(2) Frederick Winslow Taylor (1856 – 1915) was an eminent American scholar and the founder of scientific management.

The core of Taylor's system is that an enterprise *must be organized in a scientific way.* Routine production methods must give way to a balanced and sound plan. Implements should be rationally designed and placed. Work motions and techniques must also be as rational as possible and therefore have to be scrutinized, time-studied and analyzed in order to remove all unnecessary elements. A workman should be issued a special instruction card that precisely sets the speed of work, its amount and quality. Special planning departments first proposed by Taylor as the headquarters of a business prepare these cards and determine output standards, in other words, the famous *"task"* that he referred to as one of the *pillars* of his system. A man who fails to perform his task loses his bonus, a second failure leads to his discharge.

This *bonus* is the *second pillar* of Taylor's system that incorporated a differential piece rate and a bonus scheme.

The next principle is the careful selection of men for a particular job.

Finally, one of the cornerstones of Taylorism is the idea of functional management that involves a number of foremen (teachers) responsible for particular production functions.

Taylor's system, therefore, was geared to streamlining all the factors of production in order to achieve the best results with the least expense of energy and materials.

Taylor denied the idea of the irreconcilable conflict between labor and capital. On the contrary, he believed they shared common interests. He thought of his management system and theory as a source of future prosperity, since its main goal was, in his own words, "to secure the maximum prosperity for the employer, coupled with the maximum prosperity for each employee." He reminded his opponents that "prosperity for the employer cannot exist through a long term of years unless it is accompanied by prosperity for the employee, and vice versa."

Such declarations, however, should not be taken at face value. Taylor's critics reasonably accused him of pursuing maximum efficiency *at any price,* primarily due to unsustainable intensification of labor and total that many workmen just could not sustain, and a complete lack of regard for the human factor. At the same time, we cannot ignore the fact that Taylor was the first to systematize the best management practices that humanity had accumulated over the centuries and proposed fundamentally new organizational forms, principles and methods that promoted management to a *scientific discipline.*

His management system was a major success in the USA and later spread to the entire industrial world.

In Russia, the spread of Taylorism, however, was strongly affected by the 1917 revolution. Let us discuss this issue in greater detail.

Classical Taylorism started making its way into Russia somewhat later, in 1908-1909, to experience a true boom in 1911-1914. Taylor's ideas were enthusiastically discussed by students, professors, economists, journalists, engineers, and politicians. Numerous papers and magazines readily published articles on this topic; even a special publishing house was established, with Levenstern, an engineer, as its director. Note that during this period all the principal works by Taylor and other founders of scientific management (Gilbreth, Gantt and more) were translated into Russian.

Even more significant was that as of 1912, as evidenced by Gastev, efforts to introduce scientific management practices at a number of plants, notably the Aivaz machine-building factory that had been built in Saint-Petersburg with the use of state-of-the-art European technology and management principles, the Volcano factory, Semenov's factory, an artillery cannon factory, Southern railways and some others. Prior to World War I, Russia had 8 enterprises using Taylor's system compared to only one in France.

Regrettably, power in Russia was seized by Bolsheviks headed by Lenin who as early as in 1913 branded Taylorism a ruthless system of exploitation "squeezing sweat out of workers." The progress of scientific management in the country stopped from 1917 till 1920. Just a few principles of scientific management were occasionally used in a simplified form at certain military factories. However, once the civil war was over and the country moved to the "new economic policy" (1921) the movement for scientific organization of labor gained new momentum.

A landmark event in this context was the First All-Russian Initiating NOT Conference convened by the Railway Commissariat on the initiative of L.D. Trotsky on January 20, 1921. Its formal organizer notwithstanding, the conference discussed numerous issues well beyond those of railway transportation, as evidenced by papers from A. Bogdanov, V. Bekhterev, A. Gastev, M. Vasiliev, O. Yermansky, M. Falkner-Smith, S.Strumilin, G. Chelpanov and others. These presentations focused of such "non-transport" areas as industrial labor management, economic planning, labor psychology and physiology and, of course, Taylorism. With the totalitarian "war communism" system being replaced with new labor and management policies, all these issues needed to be addressed theoretically as well as practically.

The conference was attended by 313 delegates including prominent scholars such as A. Bogdanov, V. Bekhterev, A. Gastev, M. Vasiliev, O. Yermansky, G. Chelpanov and S. Strumilin, among others. Its proceedings were published in six hefty volumes.

These materials testify to substantial disagreements among the delegates with regard to NOT theories, *particularly Taylorism.*

Two opposite camps emerged during these discussions, namely Taylorists and Anti-Taylorists. The first group (I. Kannegisser, V. Nesmeyanov, N. Gredeskul and others) tended to equate Taylorism with scientific management at large, claiming that Taylor's concepts are fundamentally irrefutable as well as universal, since they cover *all* NOT problems and may essentially be accepted in their entirety under any social and economic system.

The second group (A. Bogdanov, O. Yermansky, V. Bekhterev, P. Yesmanskiy and others) vehemently rejected the idea that Taylorism was politically and ideologically neutral. They argued that Taylor's system cannot be equated with scientific organization of labor because, as Lenin noted, it aimed at intensification of labor beyond human capacities, which ostensibly ran contrary to the values of the new Russian regime.[84] Unfortunately but predictably, the second position prevailed.

(3) Henry Ford (1863 – 1947) was an American industrialist and the founder of the automobile industry in the USA. In 1892-93 he designed the first car with a four-stroke engine; his Ford Motor Company, founded in 1903, became one of the largest car manufacturers in the world.

Ford was also an outstanding pioneer of scientific management. At his factories he introduced a proprietary mass production system based on standardization, unification and the use of assembly lines. His goal was to create a car that anyone could afford. He reached this goal as early as in 1913, when his first moving assembly line was launched. From 1913 till the end of 1928, i.e., for over 15 years, Ford cars accounted for more than a half of all cars sold in the USA.

As the design of assembly lines was improving, they made way into other key industries. The Ford Motor Company used it to manufacture aircraft and, at a later point, Liberty class ships. During periods of hard work the whole ship could be assembled and welded in a mere 8.5 hours.[85]

Mass production and the economies of scale, Duncan notes, were a resounding success and a great way to supply mass markets. The assembly line had such a profound effect on humanity that it is often ranked among the greatest achievements of technology such as the nuclear bomb, the

---

[84] See more on this issue in the following chapters.

[85] See: Duncan W. J., Great Ideas in Management. Jossey-Bass Publishers. San Francisco-Oxford, 1990.

telephone, computers, TV, plastics, aircraft, guided missiles and robots.

The Ford Motor Company managed to keep its leading position for just over 10 years; in the late 1920s it lost most of its market share to competition, notably General Motors. Nevertheless, Henry Ford's achievements were nothing but brilliant.

(4) Henri Fayol (1841-1925) was a prominent French management scholar and managing director of a major mining company, who developed his own theory of administration that was vastly different from Taylorism. So long as the protagonist of this book was branded nothing else but "a Russian Fayolist" in his home country (in a highly derogatory context), we feel it would be sensible to dwell on Fayol's theory in somewhat greater detail.

Fayol published his main book, "Administration, industriélle et générale" in 1916, at a venerable age of 75. The treatise was intended to consist of four parts; however, only two of these (slightly over a hundred pages) appeared in print. In 1923, this book was published in Russia with a foreword by A. K. Gastev.

According to Fayol, all industrial activities may be divided into 6 basic groups:

1. technical activities (manufacturing, processing, treatment),

2. commercial activities (sales, purchases, barter),

3. financial activities (search for and optimum use of capital),

4. security activities (as applied to property and personnel),

5. accounting, reporting, statistics-related activities,

6. managerial activities.

Managerial activities, as we see, are listed as one of the main types of industrial activities. Fayol believed it was a sophisticated function consisting of five crucial elements: planning, organizing, commanding, coordinating, and controlling.

Planning is "to assess the future and make provision for it". Any plans must be based on real resources of the organization and possible future trends. Planning, as the most challenging and critical element of management, must involve every employee. It should be based on criteria such as integrity, continuity, flexibility (to allow for unforeseen circumstances) and precision.

Organizing is needed to supply everything a company requires in terms of "raw materials, tools, capital and personnel". Fayol pays special attention to the organizational structure of a company and its dependence on the number of personnel. More personnel necessitates additional levels of control and the formation of a scalar chain. He points out that each new group of 10, 20 or 30 workers needs a foreman; two, three or four such foremen require a dedicated manager; two or three managers require a division chief. The scalar chain, therefore, extends to the highest level of command; Fayol believed that every new manager should have no more than four to five subordinates.

The object of **command** is "to get the optimum return from all employees for the sake of the entire company". The art of command rests on certain personal qualities and knowledge of general principles of management. Fayol makes the following recommendations to managers:

1. Get a good knowledge of your personnel.
2. Remove incompetent staff.
3. Be familiar with all contracts between the company and its employees.
4. Be a good example.
5. Conduct periodic reviews of the body corporate with the help of summary diagrams.
6. Hold meetings with your close associates to provide uniform direction and coordination of efforts; use

written as well as oral reports.
7. Do not go into excessive detail.
8. Aim at making unity, energy, initiative and loyalty prevail among the personnel.

Coordination means maintaining harmony among various activities of the organization to balance, say, income and expenses, manufacturing and sales, inventory stock, and disposal and so on.

Finally, *control* is verifying whether everything occurs in conformity with the plan adopted and the instructions issued. Control also should point out weaknesses and errors in order to rectify them and prevent their recurrence. Apart from the basic elements or functions, Fayol also identifies the 14 principles of management that had played a major role in his own career:

1. Division of work "to produce more and better with the same effort".

2. Authority as "the right to give orders and the power to exact obedience".

3. Discipline, i.e., *"obedience, application, energy, behavior and outward marks of respect observed in accordance with standing agreements between the firm and its employees."*

4. Unity of command: "Workers should receive orders from only one manager." Double orders, a rather common occurrence, are a source of "stress, embarrassment and conflict."

5. Unity of direction: "Group efforts on a particular plan should be led and directed by a single person". Fayol argued that "this fulfills the principles of unity of command and brings uniformity in the work of the same nature. A two-headed body in the social as well as in the animal word is a monster that usually does not survive."

6. Subordination of individual interests to general interests: "The interest of the business enterprise ought to come before the interests of individual workers." Coordination of business interests and individual interest is one of the greatest practical challenges for a manager.

7. Fair remuneration: Wage-rates and method of their payment should be fair, proper and satisfactory. "The employer must take care of his personnel's health, fitness, education, morale and stability....even outside of the factory, and act wisely to improve their general level of education and development without infringing on their personal freedom."

8. Centralization as "something inherent to the natural order of things. In any social or animal organism feelings converge in the brain or another directing organ that sends commands to all parts of the organism to set them into motion."

9. Scalar chain is "the chain of superiors ranging from the ultimate authority to the lowest rank."

10. Order. According to Fayol, "there should be safe, appropriate and specific place for every article" (physical order) as well as "a specific position for every person and a person to fit every position" (social order).

11. Equity as a combination of justice and kindness that requires "reason, experience and good humor... without forsaking discipline."

12. Stability of personnel. "High personnel turnover is both a symptom of an ill-functioning enterprise and a reason for its poor performance."

13. Initiative is primarily the ability to draw up plans and ensure their implementation. Fayol argued that management should give all employees an opportunity to propose their new ideas by delegating some of its power.

14. Team spirit ("esprit de corps") is the fostering of harmony in an organization. "Sowing discord among employees is an unworthy business of talentless people. A true talent means good coordination of efforts among all workers, who receive a decent pay that causes no jealousy from others and does not damage harmony at the enterprise."

This the essence of Fayol's theory that sparked, much like Vitke's works, most toxic and undeserved criticism from Rozmirovich and other hack experts in the field of management. In fact, in the first quarter of the 20th century,

Fayol was probably the only scholar in Europe who could be compared to Taylor.

(5) For readers who had no chance to see the first volume in this series (a book about Gastev) we reproduce an excerpt about Yermanskiy.

Yermanskiy Osip Arkadievich (1866 - 1941) - one of the leading pioneers of the Russian labor science, professor, author of the "physiological optimum" concept. His political views were close to Menshevism, although officially he quit the Menshevik Party in 1921.

Yermanskiy's political position inspired ferocious criticism from Communist NOT scholars. It was perhaps the main reason why this once popular figure was forgotten. At present it is mentioned rarely, even in the special literature, and usually in a negative context.

This furious criticism was initiated by Lenin who reviewed Yermanskiy's book "Scientific organization of labor and the Taylor system" (Gosizdat, 1922) in a scathing article "A fly in the ointment."[86] In his typical style ("on the one hand, the book could be a textbook, but on the other hand, it cannot..."), Lenin, although welcoming this publication, claimed it was useless because of the "fly in the ointment" such as the author's "loquacity".

It seems the true meaning of Lenin's review cannot be fully grasped without considering a rather "spicy" episode involving him and Yermanskiy back in the beginning of the 20th century at the Stockholm Joint Congress of the Russian Social-Democratic Labor Party (RSDLP). Votes cast in the election of the Presidium of the Congress turned out to be split equally between the two. In the runoff Yermanskiy saved Lenin's appointment by refusing to vote for himself. Lenin did cast his ballot for himself and won the race with 60 votes vs. 58 votes for Yermansky.[87] Apparently, the leader had never forgiven the rival his popularity that was comparable to Lenin's own.

---

[86] Lenin V.I., Complete Collected Works. V.45. P. 206-207.
[87] Yermanskiy O.A., Memoirs. *[Iz perezhitogo].* M.; L., 1927. P. 6.

Let us start our discussion of Yermanskiy's concept by noting that he was among the first Russian scholars who undertook a deep critical analysis of Western scientific management theories, primarily the Taylor system. Suffice it to say that his "Scientific organization of work and the Taylor system" was reprinted four times in Russia and translated in several other countries, including Germany.

According to Yermansky, who shared Bekhterev's views, Taylorism clearly has positive and negative aspects that are "in flagrant antagonism" with each other. The positive part, or the front side of the coin, contains the principles of truly scientific organization, whereas the negative part contradicts them completely. This is why, Yermanskiy maintained, scientific management in general cannot be reasonably equated with Taylorism. Unfortunately, the author continued, such equation is typical of many Russian scientific management scholars fascinated with Taylor's principles.

What is the right vantage point to impartially assess Taylor's system? Yermanskiy thought that such an assessment required drawing a border between the two main qualities of labor, namely **productivity** and **intensity**. [88]

Yermanskiy bet on the first quality as the only key to the bright future of scientific management and "a more vibrant and profitable industry." Humanity owns all its progress, he noted, "to increased productivity, improved technologies and innovation aimed at the highest output possible with the least effort."

Labor intensity is another matter. While certainly leading to "the highest output possible," it takes little advantage of new means of production and better management. Rather, its effect is due only to the increase in "the *amount* of energy spent on work in an *unchanged technological environment*," i.e., due to more **strenuous** work.

---

[88] Yermanskiy O.A., Positive and Negative Aspects of Taylorism. *[Polozhitelnye i otritsatelnye storony teylorizma.]* Proceedings of the First All-Russian Initiating NOT Conference ... Vol. 1. Moscow, 1921. P. 65.

"This means a higher output is achieved with more rather than less effort." [89]

According to Yermansky, the Taylor system cannot be properly judged without a clear distinction between productivity and the intensity of labor. Namely, anything meant to increase productivity is good and, conversely, whatever methods designed to make labor more intensive (to "squeeze" as much energy from workers as possible) are bad. Once Yermanskiy formulates this criterion he proceeds to a detailed review of the positive and the negative sides of Taylorism.

On the bright side, the Taylor system is designed to achieve the best results with the least expenditure of energy and materials. The actual application of this principle, however, is thwarted by the dark side of that same system.

For instance, the very first pillar of Taylor's system is the notorious "task". In fact, this "task" should be based on a careful study of each trade, each operation and technique invoking physiology, psychotechnics, reflexology, and other disciplines. As for Taylor, he determines it using utterly non-scientific means. Time and motion studies, for example, can only record the length and duration of an operation or a motion but involve no analysis.

What does it mean to "analyze" a motion? Yermanskiy's answer is "to reveal the interdependence among the elements of a complex phenomenon." The stopwatch cannot do this. Time studies involving large numbers of workmen help select the *fastest speed* of the entire operation and make it *mandatory for all workers.* This, however, "is nothing else but mere intensification of labor that has little to do with the analysis aimed at streamlining work motions." Yermanskiy approvingly quoted Frey who said Taylorism was a way of robbing the worker of his energy to the last ounce without any regard to fatigue. No wonder, he adds, that in each of his books Taylor holds that time studies should involve "the strongest, first-class workmen."

---

[89] Ibid.

Taylor never cared to ask himself *whether the output prescribed by his system is compatible with physiological limits.* Meanwhile, Yermanskiy's calculations (willingly or not, he makes no mention of the methodology used, which makes these results rather questionable) indicate that Schmidt, the famous Taylor's pig iron handler, spent 837,000 kilogram-meters of energy a day instead of the normal 127,000 or the maximum permissible 260,000! "What we are facing here," Yermanskiy exclaimed, "is the predatory consumption of workmen's energy. It is generally typical for Taylor to take care of saving on the use of *dead matter* such as machinery and implements to achieve the *highest* results with *minimum* spending. When it comes to the *live workforce,* however, Taylor is all into *excessive* energy spending." [90]

Following Yermanskiy's reasoning, we may note that the author is generally right about the bright and the dark sides of Taylor's system but his assessment of these two sides is highly asymmetric. While he obviously belittles the positive aspects of the system, his criticism of the negative aspects is an even more obvious case of overkill. On the other hand, it is exactly this overkill that earned Yermanskiy many a flattering word from Lenin in the above-mentioned review as the "ointment".

Now let us see what Yermanskiy had to offer instead of Taylorism that he so strongly recommended not to confuse with the "scientific organization of labor."

I must say that Yermansky, much like Taylor whom he criticized, interpreted the idea of "scientific organization" in a broad way. In his opinion it covers *all* factors of production: machines and implements, their appropriate placement and use, technological processes and their improvement, the live workforce and its sound use, as well as the administration system. [91] Yermanskiy never challenged the idea of human

---

[90] Ibid., p. 68-69.

[91] Yermanskiy O.A., Work and Rest. The Problem of Fatigue. *[Trud i otdykh. Problema ustalosti.]* Proceedings of the First All-Russian Initiating NOT Conference ... Vol. 1. Moscow, 1921.

labor as a *declining factor of production* due to the steady growth in the technical and organic composition of capital, yet strongly believed labor to remain *the backbone of industrial life.* Machines and instruments, however perfect, are still created by man. Since they make physical work easier but cause ever-increasing stress and demand a greater intellectual effort, they demand a higher quality workforce where each man "should be not only a conscious "cog" of his industrial enterprise, but also a conscious contributor in economic development and public life at large." [92]

As we see, Yermanskiy's concept of various factors subject to "scientific organization" does not differ much from Taylor's. However, the Russian scholar gives unconditional priority to the human factor. If Taylor's workman is just a "cog" in the giant flywheel of the enterprise who blindly obeys his instruction card, Yermanskiy thinks of the workman as a "conscious cog" and, moreover, an active contributor to production and public life.

Hence, in contrast to Taylor, Yermanskiy thought that scientific management must first and foremost maintain the high quality of the workforce and guarantee its judicious (as opposed to "predatory") use without any "over-fatigue and exhaustion." Yermanskiy stressed it was the principal question of "whether scientific organization of labor should exist at all."

Yermanskiy was amazed that Taylor and his associates dismissed the physiological laws of work and bewildered with the obvious fact that "the four kinds of material energy - mechanical, thermal, electrical and chemical - are the subject of continuous studies, while human energy used in manufacturing has not been properly researched to this day." Yermanskiy thinks this is deeply wrong. Problems such as fatigue, exhaustion or rest must be central to scientific management. Russian NOT, he argues, faces a key challenge, that is, it needs to devise a method of measuring fatigue and exhaustion, take control of relevant psychophysiological processes and introduce, *instead of the Taylor system, some*

P. 34 -35.
[92] Ibid., p. 35.

truly scientific organization of labor that would be alien to unsustainable intensification.

Yermanskiy's reasoning about the fundamentals of scientific organization of labor is also of interest. While defining scientific management as the theory of the best or optimal use of all kinds of energy and all factors of production, Yermanskiy identified its three basic principles or laws:

1. the law of the organizational sum,

2. the principle of positive selection,

3. the optimum principle.

The first law, originally suggested by A.A. Bogdanov rather than Yermansky, is that an organizational sum exceeds the arithmetic sum of its components.

This becomes possible only if all the material and human elements of production agree with each other in accordance with the positive selection principle. In industry this means selecting the most appropriate implements (in terms of design, weight and shape) and the most appropriate man (in terms of character and physical fitness) for a particular job.

However, these two principles, according to Yermansky, are subordinate to the overarching **optimum principle.** [93]

The physiological optimum is the core of Yermanskiy's concept. He can be credited with raising a crucial and still important issue concerning the proper criteria of sound organization of work that he believed was the principal question of scientific management theory.

The duration or speed of an operation determines the intensity of effort, he argued, but could not be used as such a criterion. Otherwise, no limits ought to be set to speed (intensity) while in fact it is curbed by the physical abilities of

---

[93] For more details see: Yermanskiy O.A., On the Criterion of Efficiency. *[O kriterii ratsionalnosti].* "Za ratsionalizatsiyu", 1928, No.2.

man. He also rejected the criterion of space, since sometimes the working organ has to cover a longer distance for greater efficiency. While rejecting time and space as criteria for sound organization, he rather regards them as "the forms taken by the phenomena of existence" including manufacturing activities.

He thought the principal elements of any manufacturing activity are the energy expended by all factors of production (E) and the useful result (R) achieved by spending this amount of energy. "An arrangement that leads to a maximum R at the expense of excessive energy consumption is obviously anything but efficient." On the other hand, the least amount of energy spent also cannot be a criterion since in this case the result may be negligible.

What, then, can apply as the only criterion of management efficiency? Yermanskiy thought it was the ratio between R and E that he calls the efficiency factor or m:

$$m = R / E$$

The value m that shows the amount of useful work per unit of energy spent is the best criterion of efficiency. Managers should always strive for the greatest output possible per unit energy or for spending as little energy as possible per unit output. This is the essence of the optimum principle that Yermanskiy believed to be the heart of NOT. Any violation of this principle means that management is non-scientific since it leads to either squandering all kinds of energy or their underutilization. To achieve the greatest cost-effectiveness one needs in-depth knowledge of manufacturing processes and their human and material factors in order to combine and use them in the most efficient fashion. Apart from this, one certainly needs to know the basic rules of management and the optimum principle itself.

This is the essence of Yermanskiy's concept that was fiercely yet sometimes rather pointlessly criticized by his peers and, to his disappointment, never gained universal recognition[94].

---

[94] Yermanskiy O.A., Theory and Practice of Innovation. *[Teoriya*

Its main highlight, in our view, is the idea of the need to maintain productivity at an optimal, evidence-based level, since deviations from the sensible norm to either side are "extremely harmful in terms of the national economy and the sound use of all resources."[95] Accordingly, the management system must ensure the normal operation of all departments and all employees.

However, this concept was not without major flaws. As A.K. Gastev noted, the author largely ignored the challenges faced by the Russian economy in the 1920s after it was all but shattered by the revolution and the war. Enormous efforts were needed to recover the economy on an advanced technological basis as soon as possible. Yermanskiy's concept in this context sounded way too idealistic. Many points he made (e.g., the need to measure energy consumption by monitoring the amount of oxygen inhaled and carbon dioxide exhaled by the worker as well as some others) seemed pretty Utopian.

Yermanskiy also vastly exaggerated the universal significance of the optimum principle, claiming it to be the sole core of scientific management. In terms of methodology, this absolutization was not very compatible with the comprehensive approach supported by Yermanskiy. He also acted in a highly intolerant way himself. In particular, he strongly criticized Gastev's "narrow base" concept as "primitive" and castigated Vitke's nascent socio-psychological analysis of management.

Again, however, no critical analysis of Yermanskiy's concepts should overshadow their undisputed value. His message to modern economists is that they should look for management and production arrangements that neither overstress nor underuse the workman so as to eventually ensure sustained productivity growth.

---

i praktika ratsionalizatsii] Moscow-Leningrad, 1925. P. XI.
[95] Yermanskiy O.A., The Criterion of Rationality. *[O kriterii ratsionalnosti.]* P. 7.

(6) Vitke read Emerson and mentioned him with respect. Moreover, he probably had at least as much influence on Vitke as Fayol. Suffice it to say it was Emerson who coined the expression "the spirit of the hive" so often used by Vitke.

Harrington Emerson was a prominent scholar and the author of a system of efficient management. He studied in the USA, Germany, Great Britain, France, Italy, and Greece; he was fluent in 19 languages and was appointed Professor of Modern Languages at the University of Nebraska at the age of 23. Instead of pursuing an academic career, however, he soon switched to management studies for a large company and provided consultation to businesses across the world.

In "Efficiency as the basis for operation and wages" (1908) Emerson brilliantly demonstrated that our poverty was mostly due to inefficient operations, labor, and management. Good incentives such as profit-sharing can improve performance for most workers. Efficiency is unattainable from overworked, underpaid, brutalized men. Efficiency means that the right thing is done in the right manner by the right men at the right place at the right time. Duncan noted that the idea of efficiency had never before been expressed so precisely.[96]

"The Twelve Principles of Efficiency" (1913) was his most outstanding achievement. In this book Emerson formulated fundamental ideas that were, in his opinion, relevant to all forms of life on Earth. Developed over millions of years, they are hardly used by man whose overall efficiency rarely exceeds one per cent of that granted by nature. Emerson's ideas about efficiency largely center on the feeling that work must be a blessing rather than a curse. To reach this goal, work should be organized according to certain principles.

Principle 1: clearly defined ideals. An efficient organization requires that every worker is aware of its values and mission.

---

[96] See: Duncan W. J., Great Ideas in Management. Jossey-Bass Publishers. San Francisco-Oxford, 1990.

Principle 2: common sense. An organization without ideals, a clear structure and common sense is doomed to be inefficient.

Principle 3: competent counsel. Managers should never rely completely on their own skills or knowledge and ignore counsel from lawyers, accountants or engineers. No manager can be competent in every activity needed for the success of a company.

Principle 4: discipline. Work for common ideals needs cooperation. In Emerson's example, "no bee appears to obey any other bee, no bee seems consciously to cooperate with any other bee, yet so perfect is the "spirit of the hive" that every bee engrossed in her special task, fatalistically acts on the instinct that all other working bees are also as busy for the common good." This is what true discipline and cooperation are all about. He adds that "Cooperation is a matter of course, not a virtue; its absence is the crime."

Principle 5: fair deal. The manager must understand that all personnel at the company share common interests. He must also be creative and fair.

Principle 6: reliable, immediate and adequate records. Such records (on output standards, price of raw materials, wage rates and so on) are indispensable for a manager who wants to assess the true situation in the company and its true efficiency.

Principle 7: dispatching, i.e., scheduling and cost calculations.

Principle 8: standards and schedules, i.e., the use of a set of rules and instructions that are universally acknowledged for a given activity. Standards and schedules are particularly important for the calculation of costs, standard output rates and bonuses.

Principle 9: standardized conditions. Emerson noted that even major US companies operate under conditions inherited from the inefficient past. As a result, schedules become optional and emergency efforts need to be taken instead of rational control.

Principle 10: standardized operations increase the likelihood of high performance.

Principle 11: written standard-practice instructions.

Principle 12: efficiency-reward to acknowledge good performance within one's competence. Standard efficiency should not be measured as a certain short-term physical exertion but rather as a proper combination of intellectual and physical efforts that leads to sustained good performance in the future.

When all the twelve principles are applied simultaneously, Emerson noted, losses can be eliminated. If a company is unaware of these principles or makes no use of them, however, efficiency simply cannot be attained.

(7) Psychotechics (vocational psychology) is a science of determining how well people are fit for a specific job. Even Taylor suspected that professional selection of personnel was critical. However, he had no profound knowledge of psychology and physiology and therefor stopped short of discovering psychotechnical methods of finding out whether an unskilled person can be trained as a lathe operator, locksmith or driver. His system dealt with workers already trained, at some expense of money and time.

The issue of professional selection of personnel was first raised in a scientific way by Hugo Münsterberg, a well-known US psychologist who suggested experimental ways of developing a methodology that would "find the men whose mental qualities make them best fitted for the work which they have to do."[97] His innovative approach to streetcar drivers' hiring and to soldier training during World War I started the application of scientific career guidance and training methods in the USA. After World War I, psychotechnics became popular in Germany (K. Piorkowsky, O. Lipman, W. Stern, G. Mede, and others), in other European countries as well as in Russia, where it was promoted by G.Chelpanov, K.Kekcheev, A.

---

[97] Münsterberg H., Psychology and Industrial Efficiency. Boston, 1913.

Rabinovich, I. Shpilreyn, N.Rybnikov and F.Dunaevskiy, among others.

Vocational psychologists realized that modern society is dominated by the ever-deepening division of labor, with hundreds of occupations and thousands of narrow professions. Each trade calls for specific human qualities such as great physical strength, dexterity, faultless eye, long-term attention, good memory for numbers, fast response and so on. Many professions require a combination of more than one quality. Clearly, to be fit for a particular trade one should possess appropriate physical and mental abilities, as well as a natural liking for the job that otherwise would be difficult and unpleasant.

"Unfortunately, - wrote Professor G.Chelpanov, one of the pioneers of Russian psychotechnics, - people that are unfit for their job often could be used elsewhere. Without much exaggeration one can say that Newtons often worked as shepherds, while those who are only good to be shepherds covet jobs that require high talents."[98]

Scientific management scholars often tended to underestimate the critical importance of vocational psychology and its methods. For instance, as we have demonstrated in the previous book, A.K. Gastev was fairly cautious in this regard, since he believed there were no limitations to training. On the other hand, Yurovskaya, a vocational psychologist, argued that training, however important, could not solve the problem of fitness for a particular job. Moreover, certain qualities such as tactile perception, precise vision or technical sharpness, let alone intellectual faculties, can be enhanced by training only to a certain extent. Also, many abilities that were found to be

---

[98] Chelpanov G., Current Problems of Industrial Psychology (*Blizhayshie zadachi psikhologii truda.*) Proc. of the First All-Russian Conference on Scientific Organization of Labor and Production, January 20-27, 1921. [Trudy 1-i Vserossiyskoy Initsiativnoy konferentsii po Nauchnoy Organizatsii Truda i Proizvodstva 20-27 yanvarya 1921 goda]. V.5, Moscow, 1921. P. 7.

inadequate in psychotechnical tests can probably not improve at all in the course of work because "the very capacity for development is limited by age."[99] The result is inadequate performance. The economy can operate at a peak capacity, other factor being equal, only if as many workers as possible are employed according to their particular physical and mental talents.

How can millions of people be properly employed in accordance with their psychophysiological features? According to psychotechnics, this requires work in three areas:

1. To identify and classify the requirements to various professions.

2. To develop a methodology of identifying personal abilities.

3. To compare these abilities to job requirements.

Unfortunately, in the 1930s psychotechnics in Russia was completely destroyed.

(8) Helmuth Karl von Moltke (1800 – 1891), a German field marshal, chief of staff for the Prussian Army, a military theoretician, a gifted commander. The actual commander-in-chief in victorious wars with France, Austria and Denmark.

(9) The First International NOT Congress (Prague, 1924) was a triumph for Russian scientific management. The Russian delegation included A. Gastev, N. Bernstein, and A. Labutin (all from TsIT), E. Rozmirovich (People's Commissariat of Workers' and Peasants' Inspectorate), I. Shpilreyn (industrial psychotechnics laboratory under the People's Commissariat of Labor), M.

---

[99] Yurovskaya M.A., Adult Intellectual Capacities and Determination of Fitness for Intellectual Work. *[Problema umstvennoiy odarennosti u vzroslykh i opredelenie prigodnosti k umstvennomu trudu.]* "Voprosy psikhofiziologii, refleksologii i gigieny truda". Issue 1. Kazan, 1923. P. 108.

Vasiliev (People's Commissariat of Transportation), and F. Noa (All-Russian Association of Engineers). Gastev made his presentation in French and Bernshteyn made his in English. The former dealt with TsIT's setup methodology, the latter with standardization of motions. Unlike other presentations, those by Gastev and Bernshteyn triggered an animated discussion. TsIT's methodology generated so much interest that Gastev and his colleagues were promptly invited to implement it at a leading European factory where a special shop would be made available. "We are far from being deluded with our success, but in any event the Congress demonstrated that our work has come to stir international interest, as evidenced, in particular, by papers on our methodology that have started appearing in Western Europe and America."[100] Indeed, the Prague congress generated a growing awareness of the "Russian school" of scientific management among foreign scholars.

(10) Ratenau, Walter (1867 – 1922), was a German industrialist and statesman, chairman of the board of the Allgemeine Elektrizitäts-Gesellschaft (AEG), an electrical engineering company (since 1915). As Minister of Foreign Affairs, he signed the Treaty of Rapallo with the Soviet Union. He was assassinated by members of the terrorist Organization Consul.

(11) Webb, Sydney (1859 – 1947) was a British economist, historian of labor movement, the ideologist of trade-unionism and «Fabian socialism», one of the founders and leaders of the Fabian society.

(12) Vitke's views were obviously under a strong influence of Ordway Tead, an American organizational theorist whose name, as evidenced by W. Duncan, is hardly mentioned in the world literature let alone Russia where his works have never been translated.

---

100 "Organizatsiya truda", 1924, No.6-7. P. 68.

Ordway Tead's main research dates back to 1920-1940s. He focused on social psychology and leadership as the principal factors of management that becomes "a social burden" if human lives are ignored. Humans should never be reduced to the level of machines or sacrificed to relentless profit-making.

A manager's principal task is to define priority goals and make them attractive to workers. Otherwise, no efficient motivation is possible. Tead referred to industrial work as "collective cooperation" and believed that common efforts to reach worthy goals give life a meaning and satisfy the aspiration for democracy. He cherished democracy as the highest value and wanted industrial relations to be planned in a democratic way to take into account the problems of workers and their cooperation.

(13) Kerzhentsev Platon Mikhailovich (1881 - 1940) was a well-known politician and statesman, economist, historian and writer. He was the Russian ambassador to Sweden and Italy, worked as Deputy Manager of the Central Statistical Agency and as the chief government censor. He also held prominent positions in the NOT movement such as member of the Presidium of the All-Union NOT Council at CCC-RKI and Chairman of the Time League. Kerzhentsev published numerous works on scientific management such as "Principles of Organization" (Selected Works. Moscow, 1968); "Struggle for Time" (Moscow, 1965), "Organize Yourself" (Moscow-Leningrad, 1927) and "NOT: Scientific Organization of Labor and Tasks of the Party"(Moscow-Petrograd, 1923).

Kerzhentsev supported Bogdanov's idea that all various forms of organization in nature, technology and society share some features and principles to be studied by a special science; his approach, however, was limited to *management processes in society* or *in human groups regardless of their activities.* Kerzhentsev believed that scientific laws apply to any type of management. Appropriate organization, he wrote, must become the cornerstone of society including not only some enterprises or industries but also the entire economy, government, the army, trade-unions and the Party, in other words, to all entities in the country. As you see, Kerzhentsev's methodology remains broad enough despite its limitations. His idea that any organizational work with people follows some general laws essentially anticipated the main principle of management in terms of *praxeology*. This approach led him to a valuable idea that management experience can be transplanted from one area to another, e.g., "military experience can be somehow used in industry, and industrial management practices can be used in cultural work and so on." [101]

According to a number of general principles formulated by Kerzhentsev, an efficient organization needs, in particular, to set its goals and objectives, to select a structure, develop a plan and a work methodology, set a policy of using physical and human resources and establish accounting and control mechanisms.

Unfortunately, Kerzhentsev was a diehard Kremlin ideologist never tired of "proving" that NOT has no future under capitalism as opposed to its boundless potential in a socialist state.

(14) Ostwald, Friedrich Wilhelm (1853 – 1932) was a famous German physicist, chemist and philosopher awarded the Nobel Prize in 1909.

(15) Lazurskiy, Aleksandr Fedorovich (1874 – 1917), a prominent Russian neuropathologist and psychologist who worked under Academician V.M. Bekhterev and developed a theory of personality and character types ("characterology").

(16) Carnegie, Andrew was a North American industrialist, a billionaire and a philanthropist who donated millions of dollars to open public libraries, universities and museums. He argued that philanthropy was a moral duty of any wealthy person, for "...the man who dies thus rich dies disgraced" and any amassed fortune ought to be returned to society.

---

[101] Kerzhentsev P.M., NOT. Moscow-Petrograd. 1923. P. 54.

(17) Hoover, Herbert Clark (1874 – 1964) was the 31st President of the United States (1929-1933) from the Republican Party.

(18) Trotsky (Bronshtein), Lev Davidovich (1879 – 1940) – a famous politician and statesman, author of the so-called "permanent revolution theory", one of the leaders of the October 1917 uprising, an excellent organizer, speaker and writer of political essays. He was People's Commissar of foreign affairs (1917-1918), People's Commissar of war (1918-1925), one of the main creators of the Red Army and its commander-in-chief during the civil war, a member of Politburo (1919-1926).

Trotsky was eventually defeated in his struggle with Stalin and assassinated in Mexico by Mercader, an agent of NKVD.

(19) Vitke refers to the Ukrainian Institute of Labor (UIL) that deserves some considerable praise. Founded and headed by Prof. F.R. Dunaevskiy, a world-renowned scientific management scholar, UIL was rated abroad at par with its peers in Western Europe.[102]

Under Dunaevskiy's guidance, UIL developed an insightful concept of organization and management based on the idea that scientific organization must be *a fully integrated system*, *"a holistic complex" rather than "a bunch of isolated actions."*[103] The lack of such a complex system, Dunaevskiy observed, was not merely a theoretical issue. Whenever the principle of integration is ignored, errors, omissions and other unpleasant surprises are in stock for the practicing manager. Dunaevskiy also supported the integration principle. In a

---

[102] See "Sistema i organizatsiya", 1925, No. 12. P. 81.
[103] Dunaevskiy F.R., Comprehensive Organization.
[Kompleksnost v organizatsii.] "Trudy Vseukrainskogo instituta truda", issue 2, Kharkov. 1928. P.4.

declaration on its research philosophy, the Kharkov team came to an important conclusion about the "fragmentary" and the "integral" approach with the difference between them, as metaphorically explained by Dunaevskiy, "about the same as that between an ignorant fanatic who proclaims a certain medicine a universal remedy, and a professional doctor who issues prescriptions based on a comprehensive examination and all the particulars of the case."[104]

UIL, therefore, came up with a *key idea of a comprehensive approach to management research.*

Numerous works by Dunaevskiy and his colleagues offer many more ideas and concepts that were substantially ahead of their time. Considering, however, that a separate treatise on this scholar will be published under this project, let us not go too fast right now.

(20) Vitke naively believed that the "ideological phase" of Russian NOT would pass with the transition to the "new economic policy", partly with the help of the reorganized RKI. Regrettably, his hopes never materialized and the "ideological" phase of NOT was to last for 70-odd years and end only with the demise of socialism in the Soviet Union.

(21) Vitke refers to Lenin's famous papers "How to Reorganize Rabkrin (a proposal to the 12th Party Congress)" and "Better fewer but better" (1923). In accordance with his propensity for "centralization", the Bolshevik leader in these papers proposed to establish a single organizational center for the entire NOT movement in the country by reorganizing the existing Workers' and Peasants' Inspectorate (RKI) and merging it with the Central Control Commission of the Communist Party into one "super-authority". In April 1923,

---

[104] The position of Kharkov Labor Institute on the Organization of Labor. *[Pozitsiya Kharkovskogo instituta truda otnositelno organizatsii truda.]* "Trudy Vseukrainskogo instituta truda", issue 1, Kharkov. 1923. P.3.

this idea was endorsed by the 12th Congress of the Communist Party. The new Commissariat headed by V.V.Kuybyshev was charged with supervising all NOT-related activities in the country.

(22) Lunacharsky, Anatoliy Vasilyevich (1875 - 1933) - politician and statesman, writer, a member of the USSR Academy of Sciences. People's Commissar of Education since 1917.

(23) This paper dates back to 1925. In 1926 SOVNOT was already abolished since it was overpowered with the enormous number of tasks.

(24) Le Play, Pierre Guillaume Frédéric (1806 – 1882) was a French sociologist, politician, a mining engineer and professor at Ecole Polytéchnique. Vitke refers to his main sociological book "European Workers" where he studies working class families and their budgets as an indicator of living standards and lifestyle. Many facts in this book are still of considerable interest.

(25) Rozmirovich, Elena Fedorovna (1885 - 1953) was a major figure of the NOT movement in the USSR, the founder and director of the country's first specialized Institute of Management Technology under CCC-RKI (IMT). She was also, as we remember, the most active and vicious critic of Vitke's theories. Her main arguments may be found in the body of the text and need not be repeated here. It seems worthwhile, however, to review and assess her own work.

Rozmirovich developed a concept called "the industrial interpretation of management" based on the idea of perceived similarity between manufacturing and management processes. Firstly, Rozmirovich claimed, these processes consist of the same elements. Secondly, manufacturing and management processes follow the same principles. [105]

The director of IMT suggested that the structure of physical labor (e.g., manufacturing) and that of intellectual labor such as management (e.g., drafting a plan or a corporate balance sheet) share many fundamental features. She defined management as "a purely technical process of coordinating and organizing the use of workforce in industry or in office work that is carried out by a certain category of people with the help of special techniques applied to groups of individuals or things." [106] She believed that management as an array of planning, supervisory, controlling and regulatory (in a broad sense) actions does not substantially differ from manufacturing.

This core principle of "industrial interpretation" *stemmed from a peculiar idea of management.* Rozmirovich thought that any management unit may be regarded as a complex machine, or a system of machines engaged in a production process "expressed physically in artifacts such as folders, orders, recorded telephone messages, index cards, files and so on."[107]

She further reasoned that research into industrial labor and the elimination of needless motions make it possible to improve and automate the manufacturing process that increasingly employs sophisticated machines organized in large systems. Accordingly, the work of machine operators boils down to a number of simple motions to control the machine. Since management is similar to manufacturing, its elements may likewise be planned and streamlined. One can break management down into individual operations, study their sequence and measure them in time and space. The management process can thus be calculated in advance and automated. Note that Rozmirovich applied this principle to all levels of management, from a factory to the entire country.

---

[105] The State Institute of Management Technology. [*Gosudarstvennyy institute tekhniki upravleniya.*] Moscow, 1928. P. 7.

[106] Rozmirovich E., NOT, RKI and the Party. [*NOT, RKI i partiya.*] Moscow, 1926. P. 209.

[107] Ibid., p. 160-161.

Thus, the mechanization of production suggested that of management, whose functions would be reduced to simple motions. By assuming that all actions of a manager ("motions") can be calculated and standardized in advance, Rozmirovich left little room for creativity. Moreover, she elaborated her concepts by arguing that mechanization, once mature, will make managerial work completely redundant, since "machines themselves will already control the worker on their own," while management would be reduced to formal supervision and automatic control, ceasing to be a special authoritative function. She maintained that "the system of managing people" would give way to "the system of managing things", and management functions would "gradually lose their authority" and finally disappear altogether, as "special functions of a special kind of people." [108]

According to Rozmirovich, the social component of management (the focus of Vitke's research) was steadily contracting and soon "nothing would be left for the administration and management ... of the collective. Here we deal with the **omnipotence** of technology that turns the administrator into nothing more than a technician."[109]

As we see, this ideology offers a rather bleak future to management that will presumably become extinct as "a special function of a special kind of people."

For the sake of fairness, let us note, however, that despite such pessimistic forecasts Rozmirovich herself made a significant contribution to certain areas of applied scientific management such as the problems of management structures, functions and principles.

How can management be made as inexpensive and simple as possible? What are the ways to streamline administrative

---

[108] Rozmirovich E., Towards Better State Governance. [*Osnovnye polozheniya po ratsionalizatsii apparata gosudarstvennogo upravleniya.*] "Tekhnika upravleniya", 1926, No.7. P. 14.

[109] Rozmirovich E., NOT, RKI and the Party. [*NOT, RKI i partiya.*] Moscow, 1926. P. 185.

processes to ensure the highest return? Rozmirovich believed **the use of technology** was the answer. Indeed, management involves a complex network of various components and can be studied in a number of contexts such as economics, law, sociology, or psychology. The technological component also plays a role so once again, research into the technological aspects of management is perfectly legitimate.

Relying on the assumed similarity between production and management processes, Rozmirovich in fact anticipated the fundamental ideas of cybernetics, the systems theory and other disciplines. It was only natural for her to advocate streamlining and automation as the means to address management issues. *Some other principles and assumptions of the "industrial" interpretation*, however, seem rather problematic. Indeed, Rozmirovich had **a fundamentally wrong answer** to two key methodological questions:

1. Is it possible to simplify management to such an extent that it could be mastered by most people like regular low-skilled trades or, in the long run, by any worker? Do we need any professionally trained managers? Can management be organized in such a way as to possibly involve simple and often semiliterate peasants or machine operators?

2. Can the technological approach to management be declared the only one valid, while others would be proclaimed false and unscientific?

Rozmirovich's affirmative answer to the first question is an obvious fallacy explained by the fact that she blindly professed Bolshevik ideas and was fanatically devoted to the letter and spirit of Leninism.

Recall Lenin's "The State and Revolution": *"All* citizens become employees and workers of a *single* countrywide state "syndicate". All that is required is that they should work equally, do their proper share of work, and get equal pay; the accounting and control necessary for this have been *simplified* by capitalism to the utmost and reduced to the extraordinarily simple operations--which any literate person can perform--of supervising and recording, knowledge of the four rules of arithmetic, and issuing appropriate receipts." [110]

These days, after so many disasters and absurdities, it is easy to see that such primitive prescriptions are fatal to the economy and management. In the 1920s, however, this tempting simplicity quickly won the hearts and minds of the masses, was picked up by many economists and rapidly replicated in hundreds and thousands of articles, collections and monographs to become a paradigm of socialist management. In the long run, of course, the idea of steady "simplification" of management functions turned out to be a spectacular failure.

Consider the second question. Can the technological approach to management be declared the only one valid, while others would be proclaimed false and unscientific? Certainly not. This intolerance ignores the distinctly social nature of management. Rozmirovich reduced manufacturing to technology and denied management any special features. Hence her hasty conclusion that management could also be treated in terms of technology. The above-mentioned false premise was conducive to new delusions.

While running to extremes, the director of IMT tried to demonstrate that there was no social aspect in management. Since this was impossible without sinning against the truth, however, Rozmirovich went to the next step by admitting the social dimension of management and the need to control groups of people only under capitalism, a system that ostensibly needed to crush the workers' class resistance using a variety of economic and socio-psychological methods.[111] Under socialism, "no conflict of interests between workers and employers can exist." [112] Rozmirovich used this contrived ideological concept to prove that any research into any socio-economic problems of management was not needed.

---

[110] Lenin V.I., The State and Revolution. Collected works, 4th edition. V. 25. P. 445.

[111] Rozmirovich E., NOT, RKI and the Party. Moscow, 1926. P.198.

[112] Ibid.

Unfortunately, her passion for the technological approach entailed aggressive intolerance to any views other than her own. In particular, her voice notably stood out in the large chorus of critics who attacked Vitke's remarkable concepts. Due to her efforts, the discussion soon moved from science to politics, so Vitke had no chance whatsoever. In fact, Rozmirovich killed a promising trend in management theory using illegal weapons – that in a few years would in fact be turned against herself...

(26) Bukharin, Nikolay Ivanovich (1888-1938) was an eminent politician and statesman, a member of the Academy of Sciences. In the late 20s he opposed the extreme measures used in collectivization and industrialization. This position was declared "the right-wing deviation" from the Bolshevik party line. He was shot in 1937 and posthumously exonerated.

(27) A short note on Bogdanov is reproduced for those readers who missed the first book in the series, that on A.K. Gastev.

Bogdanov, Aleksandr Aleksandrovich (1873 - 1928) was an outstanding economist, philosopher, natural scientist, physician, writer and professor of Moscow State University. Bogdanov could break new ground in any theoretical of practical area touched by his powerful intellect. For instance, in his medical capacity he was the founder and head of the world's first Institute of Blood Transfusion. While strictly forbidding his staff to conduct risky blood transfusion experiments on themselves, he made the only exception for himself. The twelfth experiment proved fatal.

Our project includes a separate book on this outstanding person. Nevertheless, let us dwell briefly on his exceptional contribution to Russian scientific management. His principal brainchild was a concept he called **tectology, or the universal organization science.**

Bogdanov believed the issue of organization included three components, that is, things, people and ideas, and could not be handled by means of historical wisdom or organizational talents alone. He endeavored to systematize the enormous organizational experience of humanity and equip leaders with the knowledge of the relevant laws. He also maintained that the art of organization had always existed, in contrast to the science of organization. Therefore, most achievements in management died with the achiever, a talent, or a genius, and just a tiny fraction of them survived by turning into a tradition.

What should be the subject of organizational science? According to Bogdanov, it should study general principles and laws that govern processes of organization in all areas of organic and inorganic world: physical and psychological phenomena in life and nature, in the impact of elemental forces and in conscious human activity. [113] He argued that these laws exist in technology (organization of things), economy (organization of people) and ideology (organization of ideas). Thus, "the paths of nature's spontaneous creativity as well as the ways of conscious human organizational activity can and must be subject to scientific analysis." Until now, Bogdanov noted, these paths and methods had not been precisely identified for the lack of a universal organizational science, "whose time has come now." [114]

Bogdanov elaborated the basic concepts and methods of organizational science. In particular, he suggested the system approach for handling organizational issues and interpreted the relation between a system and its components by demonstrating that the organized whole may exceed the simple sum of its parts. [115] How do we explain his paradoxical

---

[113] Bogdanov A.A., Essays on the Universal Organizational Science. *[Ocherki vseobshchey organizatsionnoy nauki.]* Samara, 1921. P.11.

[114] Ibid., p.11.

[115] An average Arab soldier in single combat is no worse than an average French soldier, noted Bogdanov. However, a detachment of 200 French soldiers is in fact stronger than that of an Arab unit of 300-400 men, and a French army of 10 thousand would defeat a local army of 30 to 40 thousand men.

assertion that a combination of activities may either decrease or increase their practical sum? Well, any activity meets a certain resistance. The whole can be greater than the sum of its parts if the process of organization causes a smaller loss to combined activities than to their combined resistances. Thus, the elements of any organization can be analyzed in terms of activities and resistances. Bogdanov claimed that any system must be analyzed in relation to its environment and to each of its elements. "The first and foremost notions of tectology refer to elements and their combinations. These elements are activities and resistances of all sorts. Combinations may be organized, disorganized and neutral. Thus, the practical sum of their elements may vary." [116]

Bogdanov also suggested a number of revealing thoughts on the structural stability of a system and its factors; the forming and the regulative mechanisms; the need to use mathematics for the analysis of organizations. He put forward the idea of "biregulators" (the dual mechanism of mutual control) similar to the feedback concept in cybernetics, introduced the principle of "chain connection", "the minimum principle" and more.

Bogdanov used his approach to make a daring and exciting attempt to create a monistic concept of the universe. Since he believed that organization was the essence of animate and inanimate nature, he in fact reduced any activity to organizational activity. In his view, humanity has no other activities besides organizational activities, no other problems, no other points of view on life and the world, except for organizational ones. The universe, Bogdanov argued, acts as an infinitely unfolding tissue of systems that feature different types and levels of organization (complete chaos simply does not exist – it is a meaningless word). The struggle and interactions among these systems form the universal organizational process that can be split into an infinite number of elements yet remaining an integral and continuous whole.

(Ibid., p.46).
[116] Ibid., p.48.

What about destructive, i.e., disorganizing activities? Bogdanov admitted to their existence but classified them as a specific kind of organizational activities. "If social classes or groups," he wrote, "clash to disorganize each other, the reason is precisely that each such class or group strives for organizing the world and humanity according to their own needs. These clashes result from the fact that organizing forces are separated and isolated, and have yet to attain a harmonious unity. They are the struggle of organizational forms."

The two main organizational mechanisms mentioned above are central to Bogdanov's concept.

The forming mechanism includes components such as conjugation (combination of complexes), ingression (when two complexes share an element) and disingression (disintegration of the complex). Let us consider these terms in greater detail.

Human organizational activity in any area, according to Bogdanov, means connecting and separating the available elements. For instance, "labor is nothing but combining various materials, implements and manpower, and removing some of their parts to arrive at the organized whole, i.e., the 'product'." [117] These two acts, the connection and the separation, do not play an equal role in human activity; the former is primary, the latter secondary. The combination of complexes (the primary moment) is the foundation of a tectological mechanism called "conjugation," a term borrowed from biology. Bogdanov's "conjugation" was a sweeping notion that covered partnership or any kind of other communication, alloying metals, exchange of goods between factories and much more (the assimilation of food, hugs and kisses, a meeting of workers, a military skirmish and so on). Complexes can unite (which leads to an organizational crisis and makes the tectological border between them disappear) to form a fundamentally different system directly, via "ingression" or the formation of a ligament. A system that consists of complexes connected by a ligament is called an ingressive system. Conjugated systems may also disintegrate into new separate entities with new borders. This process of "disingression" also entails an organizational crisis

---

[117] Ibid., p.63.

of the system, though of a different nature. "All crises observed in life and nature, - claimed Bogdanov - all "coups d'état", "revolutions", "catastrophes" and so on belong to these two types. For example, social revolutions typically break boundaries between classes; boiling water breaks the physical boundary between the liquid and the atmosphere; the reproduction of a living cell gives rise to a border between its newly independent parts and so forth." [118]

In addition to the forming mechanism "tectology" has a regulating mechanism that selects the best combination of elements. Selection, according to Bogdanov, is the only way that "forms" can survive in nature. Selection can be positive or negative; it may occur in developing complexes as well as in those suffering a relative decline. These two types of selection collectively cover all natural and social processes, and their complementary unity spontaneously organizes the world.

Therefore, Bogdanov's organizational model is a universal concept that he applied to an infinite range of processes and phenomena in both nature and society.

Bogdanov wrote that "Man in his organizing activity is only a disciple and imitator of nature as the great universal organizer. Therefore, no human method can go beyond the methods of nature and will always be just a particular instance of these methods." [119]

Bogdanov applied the principles of his universal organizational science to economic management and planning, particularly on the national scale. In fact, this was the subject of his presentation at the First All-Russian NOT Conference. The development of a plan, he claimed, critically depends on the understanding of functional chain connections between various sectors and therefore should take into account the tectological "law of the least." In his own words, according to this law "the strength of a chain is determined by the weakest of its links; the speed of a squadron by its slowest vessel; the yield of crops by the factor least favorable to the harvest

[118] Ibid., p.75.
[119] Ibid., p.63.

(Liebig's law of the minimum) and so on. According to this law, the rate of economic growth depends on the sectors that lag behind the most."[120]

Bogdanov held that this law applied to physical, mental, social and economic systems alike. If, for example, the output of iron grows by 5%, he wrote, all the industries that depend on it through a chain connection, can only grow by 5% - for otherwise they would be short of iron; and if they grow by less than 5%, a certain part of iron would be redundant. Similarly, industries that supply raw materials and technology for the production of iron must produce 5% more than previously.[121]. This is why economic processes also obey the law of the least.

Some authors claimed this law implied "alignment with the weakest". We beg to disagree; Bogdanov was obviously right even in terms of common sense. The idea of the "weakest link in the chain" later became the basis of network planning and management that are widely used today in various fields.

Bogdanov suggested some insights concerning the law of the least in the area of industrial management. A manager, he wrote, can sustain his business in a sound way for years by means of shrewd and timely interventions. Yet a single error of judgment or an occasional lack of attention can spell disaster, like in a combat situation. On a more detailed level, that same law is responsible for the inevitable historical limitations of authoritarian organizations that wholly depend on the individual brain of "the boss" or "the sovereign," while the life of an organization is certainly a collective phenomenon. Therefore, a single short-lived small failure of an individual may deal the entire collective a severe and even fatal blow.[122] Needless to say how relevant this idea sounds today.

---

[120] Bogdanov A.A., Organizational Science and Economic Planning. *[Organizatsionnaya nauka i khozyaystvennaya planomernost']*. "Proceedings of the First Russian Conference..." V.1. P.12.
[121] Ibid.
[122] Bogdanov A.A., Essays on the Universal Organizational

The reaction to Bogdanov's "tectology" was hostile, to say the least. His organizational ideas were fiercely criticized and his very name by the late 1920s turned into an ideological stigma. The word "Bogdanovism" was perhaps the most terrible political label to be put on a scholar during "scientific" arguments.

Was there any logic behind this unfortunate and irrational rejection of Bogdanov's organizational science? We believe there were several reasons for that. First of all, Bogdanov's ideas were certainly far ahead of their time. Russian and, for that matter, global scientific management obviously had not advanced enough to appreciate these ideas even at an elementary level. Similar works by Bertalanffi, Wiener and others were published much later and welcomed by a more prepared scientific community. Secondly, Bogdanov presented his tectology in a highly sophisticated language replete with philosophical vocabulary, as well as specific terminology borrowed from natural sciences, which, of course, did not make it any easier for management scholars and practitioners to grasp his message. Third, the plight of the "universal organizational science" was largely affected by Lenin's circumstantial, severe and often unfair criticism of Bogdanov's philosophy in "Materialism and Empiriocriticism." This fact was deftly used by social scientists from the Kremlin in their "analysis" of tectology (incidentally, Lenin never read Bogdanov but just "gave appropriate instructions" to his comrades). Finally, Bogdanov's science was presented to the reader at a difficult time in Russia. The economy collapsed all but completely after World War I, the October Revolution and the policy of "war communism", resources were in short supply and scholars were naturally expected to develop practical guidance on how to spend as little time and resources as possible to boost economic performance. Many in this situation believed there was no need whatsoever for general theoretical concepts. While dealing with specific problems such as the smart organization of the workplace, improvements in the structure of the control system or the simplification of the workflow, these scientists, so to say,

---

Science. P. 94-95.

"overlooked" Bogdanov's organizational science. In fact, they failed to realize that a purely pragmatic approach often does not allow "to see the forest for the trees."

> It was but several decades later that Bogdanov's principal ideas (the isomorphism between various organizational structures, entropy, feedback and "chain" connections, "the law of the least", and others) resurfaced to be further developed in disciplines such as the general systems theory, cybernetics, the organizational theory or synergetics. The inherent relation of tectology to these sciences is obvious today, and Bogdanov's name now ranks among Bertalanffi, Wiener, Ashby and other equally celebrated names. Western experts agree. John Gorelik, a Canadian professor, calls tectology the first ever detailed version of the General System Theory and a forerunner of cybernetics. [123] Another Canadian professor, R. Mattessich, gives Bogdanov even more credit by claiming that he was the true father of the General System Theory rather than Bertalanffy, as is generally believed.[124]

The issues of precedence are certainly important for any national science and deserve more than the often easy-going attitude of Russian scholars. Yet even more important is the fact that Bogdanov's ideas that were burned in the bonfires of the Bolshevik Inquisition re-emerged like a phoenix from the ashes. Fortunately, such great manuscripts do not burn.

---

[123] Bogdanov A.A., Tectology: A Universal Organization Science. [Tectologiya (Vseobshchaya organizatsionnaya nauka)]. V.1. Moscow, 1989. P.13.
[124] Ibid., p.14.

About the author

Shcherbakovskiy, Grigory Zinovievich is Doctor of Economics, Professor at the Department of Economic and Social Systems Planning and Forecasting at St. Petersburg University of Economics and Finance. Mr. Shcherbakovskiy specializes in management, marketing, economic theory and history. He has authored numerous well-known monographs and papers. He lives in St. Petersburg, Russia.

Made in the USA
Middletown, DE
23 August 2018